GROUND TRANSPORTATION
PROFESSIONALS

PRACTICAL CAREER GUIDES

Series Editor: Kezia Endsley

GROUND TRANSPORTATION PROFESSIONALS

A Practical Career Guide

MARCIA SANTORE

ROWMAN & LITTLEFIELD
Lanham • Boulder • New York • London

Published by Rowman & Littlefield
An imprint of The Rowman & Littlefield Publishing Group, Inc.
4501 Forbes Boulevard, Suite 200, Lanham, Maryland 20706
www.rowman.com

6 Tinworth Street, London, SE11 5AL, United Kingdom

British Library Cataloguing in Publication Information Available

Library of Congress Cataloging-in-Publication Data

Names: Santore, Marcia, 1960– author.
Title: Ground transportation professionals : a practical career guide / Marcia Santore.
Description: Lanham : Rowman & Littlefield, [2021] | Series: Practical career guides | Includes bibliographical references. | Contents: Introduction—Why Choose a Career in Ground Transportation?—Forming a Career Plan—Pursuing the Education Path—Writing Your Résumé and Interviewing. | Summary: "Ground Transportation Professionals: A Practical Career Guide includes interviews with knowledgeable professionals in this stable, lucrative, and growing profession"—Provided by publisher.
Identifiers: LCCN 2021015947 (print) | LCCN 2021015948 (ebook) | ISBN 9781538152072 (paperback) | ISBN 9781538152089 (epub)
Subjects: LCSH: Transport workers. | Transportation—Vocational guidance.
Classification: LCC HD8039.T7 S26 2021 (print) | LCC HD8039.T7 (ebook) | DDC 388.023—dc23
LC record available at https://lccn.loc.gov/2021015947
LC ebook record available at https://lccn.loc.gov/2021015948

Contents

Introduction

So You Want a Career in Ground Transportation

*W*elcome to a career in ground transportation! If you've opened this book, you're curious about what a career in ground transportation would be like. Maybe you've always liked the idea of taking to the open road to see the country, meet new people, and maybe have a few adventures along the way. Maybe you're fascinated by the interlocking moving parts of complex systems. Maybe you don't really know what you want to do and you're wondering if ground transportation will be the right road for you.

Ground transportation offers many opportunities! *kali9/E+/Getty Images*

So what is ground transportation? There's more to it than you might think. To get an idea of the entire world of ground transportation, first you need to understand an important term: the supply chain.

Ground transportation is an essential part of the supply chain. *metamorworks/iStock/Getty Images*

The Supply Chain

What is the "supply chain," and what does it have to do with ground transportation? In a nutshell, the supply chain is the system of interconnected organizations, information, resources, and activities that work together to get products to consumers. That includes sourcing the raw materials, refining those resources into usable materials, manufacturing the product, selling the product to end users, and delivering finished products to end users or customers.

The supply chain is usually described as having five parts:

1. Sourcing or extracting raw materials
2. Refining raw materials and/or manufacturing materials into basic parts
3. Assembling those basic parts into finished products
4. Selling finished products to end users
5. Delivering finished products to end users or consumers[1]

Ground transportation is an important part of almost every one of those steps—from transporting raw materials to processing locations, to transporting processed materials to manufacturers, to delivering manufactured goods to stores, wholesalers, or directly to customers. In between each of these steps, you'll find important work going on, as described by supply chain experts Blume Global:

- Documentation, contracts, and other information that define expectations throughout the supply chain
- Physical movement of goods from one location or organization to another
- Storage of goods until they are needed
- Stock and inventory tracking and management
- Demand and supply management
- Tracking and authentication of goods
- Onward logistics and distribution of goods to the end customer[2]

Improvements in productivity and efficiency go straight to the bottom line of a company and have a real and lasting impact. Good supply chain management keeps companies out of the headlines and away from expensive recalls and lawsuits.—Kristina Zucchi[3]

Careers in Ground Transportation

Careers in ground transportation span every aspect of the supply chain—all the ways we move things from one place to another. Ground transportation also includes all the ways that we can move people one place to another. So a career in ground transportation could be everything from driving a cab to driving a semitruck to managing the flow of materials and manufactured products until they reach their final end user.

There are many careers in ground transportation that are available to someone with a high school diploma. Other opportunities open up with more experience and/or more education. Take a look at the careers covered in this book—it's a great starting point to learn more about your options in the world of ground transportation.

What Does This Book Cover?

In this book, you'll get a general overview of different types of careers in ground transportation that are essential for keeping goods or passengers moving from one part of the country to another. There isn't room in this guide to consider the entire railroad system, so we stick to ground transportation that uses roads and highways.

CHAPTER 1: WHY CHOOSE A CAREER IN GROUND TRANSPORTATION?

In the first chapter, you'll learn about certain ground transportation jobs, what they are, what they do, what they pay, and what you can expect in these careers. First, we take a look at jobs that involve transporting individual passengers or groups of passengers:

- Taxi drivers
- Chauffeurs
- Ride-hailing drivers
- Local transit bus drivers
- Intercity bus drivers
- Charter bus drivers
- School bus drivers
- Paratransit van drivers

Then we look at the people who transport goods around town or across the nation:

- Local truck drivers
- Regional truck drivers
- Long-haul truck drivers

Finally, we take a look at who is working off the road to see the big picture, analyze the data, and plan the best, most efficient, and most cost-effective way to move goods throughout the supply chain:

- Distribution/supply chain managers (logisticians)
- Supply chain engineers
- Other supply chain careers

CHAPTER 2: FORMING A CAREER PLAN

The second chapter is all about you and how you can plan your career in ground transportation. What do you need to know about yourself? What kind of ground transportation career suits you best? How can you make your time in high school work for you? Where can you find more information?

CHAPTER 3: PURSUING THE EDUCATION PATH

The third chapter shows you what kind of education or training you need for each ground transportation career. You'll learn what to consider when choosing your educational opportunities, how admissions and financial aid work, and some things to watch out for.

CHAPTER 4: WRITING YOUR RÉSUMÉ AND INTERVIEWING

In the fourth chapter, you'll learn about applying for and keeping a job in ground transportation. You'll learn about applications and résumés, interviewing, and how to put your best foot forward.

> Afoot and light-hearted I take to the open road,
> Healthy, free, the world before me,
> The long brown path before me leading wherever I choose.
> —Walt Whitman, "Song of the Open Road"[4]

Where Do You Start?

There are a lot of options in the field of ground transportation. Which one will be right for you? Discover the path you want to take by turning the page and taking the first step.

Get ready to push "Go" on your ground transportation career! *Olivier Le Moal/iStock/Getty Images*

Why Choose a Career in Ground Transportation?

About Ground Transportation

*G*round transportation can include any kind of conveyance that carries goods or people over land. Some ground transportation involves carrying passengers. That could include taxis, limousines, and ride-share services (like Uber or Lyft) that take individuals from one place to another. It could mean school buses, local transit buses, or intercity or charter buses that take groups of people to and from more distant locations.

Careers in ground transportation have something for everyone. *Smederevac/iStock/Getty Images*

Another kind of ground transportation involves moving goods, supplies, or raw materials as part of the supply chain (read about the supply chain in the introduction). This includes small and medium-sized trucks that transport goods locally and regionally, as well as big rigs that transport everything from milk to gasoline to livestock to frozen foods to furniture to factory equipment across the nation.

Drivers operate the vehicles that are at the heart of ground transportation. But there are other important roles as well. That includes the people off the road who analyze the movement of people and goods and who make decisions about the best, most efficient, safest, and most cost-effective ways to keep these systems operating.

Jobs in Ground Transportation

Let's take a look at a few of those possible careers, starting with those who carry passengers, then those who carry freight, and finally the people who figure out how to make it all work. We'll start with those careers that don't require a college degree, followed by those that do.

TRANSPORTING PASSENGERS

There are many different types of ground transportation jobs that involve transporting people from one place to another. Sometimes it's a large group, and other times it's just one passenger. In all cases, these drivers are responsible for the safety of their passengers, the condition of their vehicle, and making sure the experience is a positive one for all.

Taxi Drivers, Chauffeurs, and Ride-Hailing Drivers

Taxi drivers and chauffeurs drive individuals to and from wherever they are going, like work, the airport, a hotel, shopping, or any other location. These driving jobs have certain things in common but differ in some important ways. For instance, they must all have a good working knowledge of the layout of their town or city and know the most efficient routes. They must obey all traffic laws, help passengers with their luggage, keep their vehicles clean inside and out, and keep a record of how many miles they've traveled. It's also very important to stay alert. Most injuries to these kinds of drivers come from traffic accidents, as well as from lifting heavy luggage.

Important qualities for these kinds of drivers include the following:

- Customer-service skills
- Dependability
- Eye–hand coordination
- Initiative
- Patience
- Good eyesight
- Good reflexes
- Good driving record

Taxi Driver

Taxi drivers are also called cabdrivers (or cabbies). They can be independent operators or work for a taxi company. Depending on their location, taxi drivers may pick up customers who wave at them (hailing), wait at a taxi stand (e.g., at the airport or train/bus station), or call the central dispatcher at the taxi company to say where and when they need a ride. Some cab drivers work for a

Driving a taxicab to move individuals around the town. *NadejdaReid/E+/Getty Images*

taxi company, some lease a taxicab from a dispatch service, and some own their own cabs. Taxi drivers generally work with little supervision. They can work full or part time and can take breaks whenever they don't have a passenger. Some work during normal daytime working hours; others work evening and weekend shifts.

Chauffeur

Chauffeurs drive limousines, vans, or private cars. They may work for a limousine service, a car service, a private business, a government agency, or an individual. Chauffeurs drive passengers on prearranged trips, which could be for someone going out for a night on the town or a group of high school seniors going to the prom. In some cities, it's not unusual for people who don't drive or own cars to establish a regular relationship with a car service, and often with a particular driver, to take them where they need to go. Other chauffeurs drive large vans between airports or train stations and hotels—they may be employed by a limousine company, shuttle service, or by a hotel.

Chauffeurs drive passengers on prearranged trips—sometimes in luxury! *Jacob Wackerhausen/ iStock/Getty Images*

Chauffeurs need to provide excellent customer service, especially if they drive luxury vehicles for wealthy or important people who demand a high level of service and discretion. Chauffeurs employed by individuals may find that their duties expand into something like a personal assistant.

Chauffeurs' schedules are more structured than those of cabbies or ride-hailing drivers. They remain on-call at specific times but must be ready to respond to clients' needs at a moment's notice. Chauffeurs making a regular run between a hotel and the airport, for instance, might have a particular schedule—every twenty or thirty minutes or every hour, for example—or they might need to respond to a call from the customer or hotel concierge. Those driving a stretch limousine for special occasions, such as a wedding, generally have appointments set up weeks to months in advance.

Ride-Hailing Driver

Most people call services like Uber and Lyft "ride sharing," but the technical term is "ride hailing" ("ride sharing" actually means things like carpooling). One of the main differences between ride-hailing drivers and cabbies or chauffeurs

Ride-hailing services like Lyft and Uber are sometimes called ride sharing. *adamkaz/E+/Getty Images*

is that ride-hailing drivers use their own vehicles. They work as independent contractors for the company (not employees) and must maintain their own insurance, tax withholding, health insurance, and such. (There are other companies besides Uber and Lyft, but these two are the most well known at the time of writing.) Passengers "hail" a ride by using an app on their cell phone; all financial transactions are handled through the app, so the driver never has to deal with collecting or carrying money.

Because ride-hailing drivers are independent contractors, they can set their own hours depending on their availability, preferences, and financial needs. Some of these drivers work part time as extra side income in addition to their jobs, some have retired from other jobs, and some work full time and maintain regular working hours. Because ride-hailing services often charge different rates for busier or less busy times of day, some drivers only drive at the busiest times of day in order to maximize their per-ride income.

TIPS ON TIPS

Driving a cab or limousine is one of those jobs where it's usual for the customer to give the driver a tip in addition to the cost of the fare. How much that is depends on what's usual in your location. If you drive a cab in New York City, for instance, you could expect a 15 or 20 percent tip on top of the fare.

Don't forget that tips are at the customer's discretion. You're more likely to earn a higher tip if you do the following:

- Treat the customer with respect. That doesn't mean groveling—it means being helpful and reasonably friendly. Think about how you'd like to be treated if you were the customer. Answer questions and don't roll your eyes. Don't rush the customer just so you can go look for another fare.
- Help with baggage without being asked.
- Know the area. That includes knowing the best route to your destination, being able to figure out where you need to be even if your GPS isn't quite right, and pointing out a few popular attractions or interesting landmarks during the ride.
- Drive directly and efficiently to the destination. Don't try to run up the meter by going blocks (or miles) out of your way. Even an out-of-towner will catch on to that pretty quickly.

Bus and Paratransit Van Drivers

There are many kinds of buses and many kinds of bus drivers. Buses range is size from small, fifteen-passenger buses to one hundred–passenger articulated buses (the kind with two connected sections) that can be sixty feet long. Drivers need special training to operate these often-awkward vehicles and keep their passengers safe.

The following is a list from the U.S. Bureau of Labor Statistics (BLS) of the general duties of all kinds of bus drivers:

- Pick up and drop off passengers at designated locations.
- Follow a planned route according to a time schedule.
- Help passengers with disabilities get on and off the bus.
- Obey traffic laws and state and federal transit regulations.
- Follow procedures to ensure passenger safety.
- Keep passengers informed of possible delays.
- Perform basic maintenance (check the bus tires, lights, and oil).
- Keep the bus clean and presentable to the public.[1]

All bus drivers need to share certain important qualities, for example, the following:

- Customer-service skills
- Eye–hand coordination
- Good hearing
- Good vision
- Patience
- Good health

Generally, all bus drivers need a CDL with a (P) endorsement (see the sidebar titled "Commercial Driver's Licenses"). You can earn your CDL on the job; if you already have a CDL, your training may be shorter. Many states require that bus drivers be at least twenty-one years old. Your license can be revoked or suspended if you've had a CDL suspended in another state, or if you've been convicted of a felony involving the use of a motor vehicle or of driving under the influence of alcohol or drugs. The Federal Motor Carrier Safety Administration (FMCSA) maintains a list of other potential violations.

School Bus Driver

School bus drivers transport kids to and from school, as well as sports, after-school programs, field trips, camps, and other events. To drive a school bus, you'll need special training to earn the (S) endorsement on your CDL.

There's a lot riding on the skills of a school bus driver. *andresr/E+/Getty Images*

Driving a school bus is an important and responsible job—a fact that is not always reflected in the pay scale for this career. School bus drivers ensure that children are safe getting on and off the bus, help children with disabilities, maintain order and safety on the bus, enforce the school system's rules, and report discipline problems to the school district and/or parents.

One of the biggest challenges a school bus driver faces is maintaining order on the bus while driving safely, alert to all the dangers on the road. In most school districts, the driver is the only adult on a bus that can hold as many as seventy students. When children misbehave on a bus (and if you've ridden a school bus, you know children misbehave on the bus), the driver can become distracted, which is a safety hazard for everyone on the bus and on the road.

Local Transit Bus Driver

Local transit bus drivers work for the local transit authority and drive buses on regular routes along city streets. Some local transit buses go out to suburban areas as well. You'll be picking up and dropping off passengers at regular bus stops along your route, usually every few blocks. Local transit bus drivers are responsible for collecting fares or checking bus passes when passengers get on the bus; answering questions about routes, schedules, and transfers; and letting the central dispatcher know about accidents or traffic problems along the route.

Local transit bus drivers get to know their "regulars." *skynesher/E+/Getty Images*

Local transit bus drivers work regular daily shifts, usually drive the same route, and don't need to do any extensive travel. Sometimes, you may be on a weekend, early morning, or late night shift.

Note: A word of caution—according to the BLS, transit and intercity bus drivers have one of the highest rates of injury of all occupations, mostly because of traffic accidents.

Intercity Bus Driver

Intercity buses transport people from one town or city to another, sometimes crossing states or even the entire country. Intercity bus drivers usually pick up passengers from a specific bus station in cities or designated bus stops in small towns or rural areas. The intercity bus driver makes sure that all passengers have a valid ticket, sell tickets when necessary, keep track of the passengers who get on or off the bus, and help load and unload baggage.

One example of a passenger bus company is Greyhound. To work as a bus driver for Greyhound, you have to meet all the federal requirements for a CDL with a (P) endorsement (see the sidebar titled "Commercial Driver's Licenses"). The company provides extensive training to be sure that you can drive this kind of vehicle. Greyhound also has their own grooming standards for bus drivers; this includes wearing a uniform and minimal jewelry, and having conservative haircuts and no facial hair. Their training program includes safety, how to use a logbook, and (most important) customer service and customer procedure.

Intercity bus drivers usually drive an assigned route. Some make a round trip and can go home after every shift; others may be away from home for several nights, depending on their assignment. Among other restrictions, the FMCSA allows no more than ten hours of driving time and no more than fifteen hours of total on-duty time before drivers must rest for eight consecutive hours.

Charter Bus Driver

Charter buses (also called motor coaches) carry groups of passengers on a planned trip, like a sightseeing tour of New England to see the autumn leaves or a high school trip to a historic location in another state.

Duties of charter bus drivers generally include making sure the climate controls are working properly, keeping the trip on schedule, helping load and

Intercity bus drivers and charter bus drivers get to see the sites while transporting passengers long distances. *Grafissimo/iStock/Getty Images*

unload luggage, making sure all the passengers are accounted for before moving on to the next stop, and sometimes acting as a tour guide.

Because of the nature of the trips, charter bus drivers sometimes stay with the passengers for the whole length of the trip, which means they could be away from home for days or weeks at a time. You may be working all hours of the day and night, on weekdays, weekends, and holidays.

Paratransit Van Driver

Paratransit vans are made to transport people with special needs, such as people with disabilities or the elderly in nonemergency situations. These vehicles usually have special equipment, like a wheelchair lift. Paratransit van drivers help passengers with boarding. They must know how to operate both the van and the specialized equipment, and make sure that it is safe and in good condition. Like school bus drivers, paratransit van drivers have a special responsibility to their passengers.

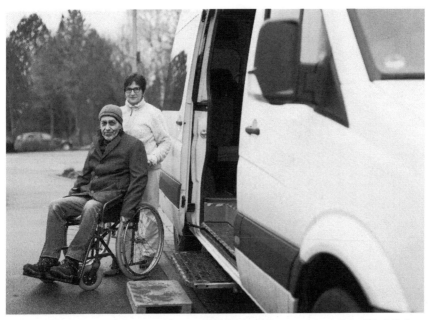

Paratransit van drivers must be great drivers and helpful to their passengers. *nullplus/iStock/Getty Images*

COMMERCIAL DRIVER'S LICENSES (CDL)

The Commercial Motor Vehicle Safety Act of 1986 mandates that anyone who drives a commercial vehicle must have a commercial driver's license (CDL). To get a CDL, you have to meet your state's residency, skills, and knowledge requirements and pass an exam. You also have to pass a medical exam and be at least twenty-one years old.

COMMERCIAL LEARNER'S PERMIT

The first step to earning a CDL is to apply for a commercial learner's permit (CLP) in your state. States have different age requirements for licensing; some allow those as young as eighteen or twenty to get a CLP (for single-state driving only), so that you will be trained and ready for your CDL when you turn twenty-one.

TYPES OF CDL

- Class A is required to drive vehicles such as tractor-trailers (aka semi, big rig, eighteen-wheeler), truck and trailer combinations, tanker vehicles, livestock carriers, or flatbeds.
- Class B allows you to operate a commercial vehicle that is not hitched to a trailer, like straight trucks, large buses (city buses, tourist buses, and school buses) or segmented buses, box trucks (e.g., delivery trucks and furniture trucks), or dump trucks with small trailers.
- Class C allows you to drive single vehicles with a gross combined weight rating (GCWR) of less than 26,000 pounds or towing another vehicle that's less than 10,000 pounds, including passenger vans, small HazMat vehicles, or combination vehicles that don't require a Class A or B license.

ENDORSEMENTS

To drive certain kinds of specialized vehicles, you will need more than just a CDL. You'll need endorsements that show you have the specialized knowledge and skill required to handle specialty vehicles.

- Passenger (P) allows you to carry passengers.
- Tank (T) lets you drive trucks containing liquid cargo.
- Hazardous Materials (H) is required to drive trucks containing dangerous substances like flammable liquids, explosives, or radioactive substances.
- School Bus (S) endorsement also requires a thorough background check.

An important note from FMCSA: "Beginning February 7, 2022, drivers applying to obtain a Class A or Class B CDL for the first time will be subject to the requirements in the Entry-Level Driver Training (ELDT) regulations. These regulations establish a Federal standard for training. CDL applicants must successfully complete this training before they will be permitted to take the CDL skills test. Drivers will search for a training provider using the upcoming Training Provider Registry. For more information, visit https://tpr.fmcsa.dot.gov."[2]

Start with your local Department of Motor Vehicles office to find out more about how to get your CDP and then your CDL.

TRANSPORTING GOODS

Goods such as raw materials, equipment, food, hazardous liquids and chemicals, and finished products are just a few of the items that are transported across the country every day in the United States. Many goods are transported by freight train, but the railroad industry is beyond the scope of this book. We will be concentrating on ground transportation of goods via roads and highways, so that means trucking.

There are many different sizes, styles, and types of truck that are used for different purposes. Based on size and configuration, these trucks fall into three categories of CDL (see the sidebar titled "Commercial Driver's Licenses"). Let's take a look through the lens of the territory you'd cover as a driver.

GROSS VEHICLE WEIGHT RATINGS

The gross vehicle weight rating (GVWR), or gross vehicle mass (GVM), is the term used for motor vehicles and trains to describe maximum operating weight or mass of a vehicle according to the manufacturer specifications. The GVWR includes the vehicle's chassis, body, engine, engine fluids, fuel, accessories, driver, passengers, and cargo but not any trailers.

Another term is gross combined weight rating (GCWR), which refers to the total mass of a vehicle including all trailers. GVWR and GCWR are used to specify weight limitations and restrictions. Gross trailer weight ratings specify the maximum weight of a trailer. Gross axle weight ratings specify the maximum weight on any particular axle.

There are two important GVWR limitations in the United States: Vehicles weighing more than 6,000 pounds (2,722 kilograms) are restricted from some city roadways. Commercial vehicles weighing more than 8,500 pounds (3,856 kilograms) must have insurance under Section 387.303 of the Motor Carrier Act of 1980.

Vehicles or combinations weighing more than 26,000 pounds (11,793 kilograms) generally require a commercial driver's license (CDL) or a non-commercial Class A or B license. A CDL is also required for certain vehicles under 26,000 pounds GVWR, such as buses and for-hire passenger vehicles that carry sixteen or more people, all vehicles transporting placarded hazardous materials or wastes (regardless of weight or load class), and any vehicle towing a trailer with a gross trailer weight more than 10,000 pounds (4,536 kilograms) where the combined weight is greater than 26,000 pounds. Laws vary by state, but typically vehicles weighing more than 10,000 pounds must stop at weigh stations.

From: https://en.wikipedia.org/wiki/Vehicle_weight.

Short-Haul Trucking: Local Delivery Driver

Local truck drivers transport goods within their own areas. This includes delivery truck drivers and driver/sales workers. They may work for a local moving company, for a specific store (such as a furniture store), or for themselves. Local truck drivers generally pick up at a local hub, deliver within their territory, and report back to the hub in the evening. Local truck drivers use a wide variety of vehicles, including the following:

- **Walk-in trucks:** Often used by delivery companies like UPS or FedEx, walk-in trucks are tall vehicles—tall enough for an adult to step in and out of the driver's compartment and walk upright through the cargo area. These are sometimes called multi-stop trucks or step vans because the driver can easily step in and out of the truck while making multiple stops.
- **Cargo vans:** These full-sized vans are different from passenger vans because there are no rear side windows and no back seats. Instead, the entire space behind the front seats is empty to make room for cargo. Commercial cargo vans should have cargo barriers that hold back the cargo in case of sudden stops or rollover accidents.

Local truck drivers make deliveries and pickups in their own area. *AnnaStills/iStock/Getty Images*

- **Box trucks:** Also known as box vans or cube trucks, box trucks have separate chassis cabs and cargo boxes, although some have doors from the cabin to the cargo area. Sometimes the rear cargo door opens upward, like a garage door. Box trucks are generally between 10 and 26 feet long (3 to 7.9 meters) and have a gross vehicle weight rating between 12,500 and 33,000 pounds.

Working Conditions

Local truck drivers have the advantage of being home every night. It's a stable job—you'll usually have a particular route that you cover over the course of a week. Sometimes you might work early or late hours, or additional hours beyond the standard forty. You'll also get to know the people you interact with on your route because you'll be seeing the same faces all the time.

Local delivery driving involves a lot of lifting, carrying, and walking, in addition to the actual driving. This results in a higher rate of injury than many other occupations.[3]

Local truck driving jobs can be harder to find than long-haul jobs (known as over-the-road or OTR jobs; see that section below) because there may not be many jobs available in the place you want to live. Even if your aim is to drive locally, you may have to put in some time on OTR jobs before the local job of your dreams is available.

Job Outlook

According to the BLS, overall employment of delivery truck drivers is expected to grow by about 5 percent by 2029, which is faster than average for all occupations. They go on to say, "Continued growth of e-commerce should increase demand for package delivery services, especially for the large and regional shipping companies. More light truck and delivery drivers will be needed to fulfill the growing number of e-commerce transactions."[4]

Short-Haul Trucking: Regional Driver

Regional truck drivers have routes that cover a particular area or region of the country. Transportation and logistics company Schneider said, "That creates

'Goldilocks' jobs that are just right for drivers still looking to hit the open road while staying close enough to home to get there weekly or more."[5]

Like long-haul truckers, regional truckers may drive an eighteen-wheeler for many days and cross state lines. Some trucks are large enough to sleep in the cabin; other times, drivers stay at hotels while they're away from home. The main difference between regional short-haul trucking and long-haul trucking is that regional truck drivers have predictable schedules and regular routes.

Truck drivers transport goods locally, regionally, nationally, and internationally. *kali9/E+/Getty Images*

Working Conditions

Regional truck drivers can balance time on the road with time at home better than long-haul truckers, while still having plenty of work. You might be away from home for a night or a few nights, but you can expect to be home on a regular basis for reasonable periods of time. Short-haul truckers are generally home every night, or at least on the weekends.

Regional truck drivers learn their routes, traffic patterns, and usual weather for the areas they cover, so there are fewer surprises that can affect safety. Rules regarding logging hours of service and using electronic logging devices are different for regional truckers than for long-haul truckers.

Job Outlook

Job prospects for regional truck drivers are very good in the 2020s, especially for Class A license holders with proper training and a clean driving record. Regional truck driving is an easier (not easy, just easier!) life than long-haul truck driving, so there isn't as much turnover or as many available jobs (see the sidebar titled "Truckers Needed!"), but there are still plenty of well-paying jobs available. In addition, many drivers are expected to retire in the near future, opening up even more opportunities for newer drivers.

TRUCKERS NEEDED!

According to the American Trucking Association, as of 2018, there was a shortfall of 60,800 truck drivers in the United States. That means not enough truck drivers to fill all the available jobs. They predict that over the next decade, the trucking industry will need to hire around 1.1 million new truck drivers (about 110,000 each year) to fill that gap and replace drivers who retire or leave for other reasons. The ATA analysis focused on drivers of Class 8 tractor-trailers, noting that "the vast majority of the shortage is within the over-the-road, or non-local, for-hire truckload sector."[6]

Long-Haul Truck Driver

Long-haul trucking is done by drivers with Class A licenses who transport goods long distances in heavy trucks and tractor-trailers (semitrucks). These trucks usually have a GCWR of 26,000 pounds or more for the vehicle, passengers, and cargo (see the sidebar titled "Gross Vehicle Weight Ratings"). They may cross many states or the entire country; they may even go into Canada or Mexico.

In addition to following the rules of the road, long-haul truck drivers are responsible for the following:

- Ensuring their cargo is loaded, balanced, and secured properly
- Inspecting their trailers before and after every trip and recording any defects
- Maintaining a log of their working hours
- Following all federal and state regulations, including those for hours of rest

This father and daughter team knows that taking turns is good for long-haul truck drivers. *Lady-Photo/iStock/Getty Images*

- Reporting serious mechanical problems
- Keeping their trucks and equipment clean and in good working order
- Reporting any incidents on the road to the dispatcher

The driver's route is usually assigned by the dispatcher, but some drivers plan their own routes. In these cases, it's important to know which roads prohibit large trucks and where highway construction or roadwork may slow down your journey.

Working Conditions

Driving a truck does not mean that you sit all day. It can be a physically demanding job, involving loading and unloading cargo and driving for many hours at a time. Driving is more exhausting than most people realize, and driving while extremely tired can lead to accidents—including fatal ones. That's why the FMCSA regulates the number of hours a long-haul truck driver can spend behind the wheel. The BLS summed up these rules as follows:

Drivers may not work more than 14 hours straight, comprising up to 11 hours driving and the remaining time doing other work, such as unloading cargo. Between working periods, drivers must have at least 10 hours off duty. Drivers also are limited to driving no more than 60 hours within 7 days or 70 hours within 8 days; then drivers must take 34 hours off before starting another 7- or 8-day run. Drivers must record their hours in a logbook. Truck drivers often work nights, weekends, and holidays.[7]

Long-haul truck drivers are often away from home for long periods of time, which can put a strain on relationships. It can be a lonely way of life. There is also a higher risk of injury than in other occupations.

Drivers who work in teams have several advantages over those who drive alone. They have company and someone to share the driving with. This means they can minimize their downtime, since one person can drive while the other sleeps. Some driving teams are married couples, which gives them more time together. Team driving also pays better than solo driving because customers will pay a higher rate to keep their freight moving and have it arrive sooner.

Job Outlook

The job outlook for heavy and tractor-trailer truck drivers is very good for those with the right training and driving record. It's a hard life, so there is a lot of turnover as drivers move from one company to another, switch to regional or local driving to be at home more, or retire. That means that there should be good jobs available for anyone who is willing to put in the hard work, time, and self-discipline that it takes to be a long-haul truck driver. See the sidebar called "Truckers Needed!" to learn more.

Distribution/Supply Chain Manager (Logistician)

Distribution managers, supply chain managers, and logisticians specialize in creating, managing, tracking, and optimizing the various links in the supply chain (see the introduction for more about the supply chain). They are part of a process that provides timely, accurate, and consistent information across a large network of businesses and organizations to identify issues and streamline the manufacturing and transportation of goods.

Distribution managers, logisticians, and supply chain managers analyze data and plan systems.
gorodenkoff/iStock/Getty Images

Investopedia defines distribution management as the "process of overseeing the movement of goods from supplier or manufacturer to point of sale. It is an overarching term that refers to numerous activities and processes such as packaging, inventory, warehousing, supply chain, and logistics."[8]

Today, supply chain and distribution management is much more than just moving things from here to there. They coordinate the logistics of every aspect of the supply chain. They work to reduce shortages and keep costs down. It involves collecting, analyzing, and sharing data and covers many complex functions, including integrating information about shipping, warehousing, inventory control, trucking/fleet operations, packaging, receiving, materials handling, and customer service, as well as planning for plants, warehouses, and stores.

To manage all parts of the supply chain, you need a good understanding of the new technologies that are being designed to make the process more transparent, more efficient, and less wasteful, resulting in better, more productive relationships with customers and end users. Some of those technologies will include the following:

- Internet of Things (IoT) devices
- Blockchain technology

- Supply chain software
- Real-time inventory
- Automation of common activities
- Data analysis and reporting
- Machine learning and artificial intelligence[9]

It's a complex job that requires you to manage many "moving parts" at the same time.

Qualities

- Ability to see the "big picture"
- Ability to keep track of fine details
- Math skills
- Communication skills
- Critical-thinking skills
- Customer service skills
- Multicultural understanding
- Ability to learn new programs, systems, and technologies quickly and correctly
- Commitment to excellence and constant improvement

Working Conditions

Most supply chain/distribution managers and logisticians work full time and sometimes put in some overtime hours to make sure everything stays on schedule. These jobs are found with large businesses, especially in manufacturing, wholesale, and retail chains. In a smaller company, distribution managers could divide their time between the office environment and the warehouse environment. In larger companies, distribution managers work more in the office, with teams helping to ensure the work is complete.

Supply chain management can mean extensive travel and on-call hours in order to work among different time zones, because company headquarters, manufacturing plants, raw material sources, shipping, and customers could be in different countries or on different continents.

There is definitely room for advancement in distribution management and logistics. It's not unusual for managers to be promoted to senior corporate positions like vice president or even C-suite positions (chief executive officer, chief operations officer, chief financial officer).

Distribution and supply chain managers work in offices, warehouses, and in the field. *gorodenkoff/ iStock/Getty Images*

Job Outlook

The BLS predicts about 4 percent job growth between 2019 and 2029, which is about the same as the average for all occupations. They add, "Overall job opportunities should be good because of employment growth and the need to replace logisticians who transfer to other occupations or leave the labor force, such as to retire. Prospects should be best for candidates who have experience using logistical software or doing logistical work for the military."[8]

Corporations are now very aware of the impact that supply chain management can have on the operations and economics of a company. This recognition has resulted in a strong total compensation package for these jobs.—Kristina Zucchi[10]

Supply Chain Engineer

Classified in the "industrial engineer" category, supply chain engineers engage in supply chain management to help businesses minimize inventory costs, conduct quality assurance activities to help businesses keep their customer bases satisfied, and work in the growing field of project management as industries across the economy seek to control costs and maximize efficiencies.[11]

Supply chain engineers use mathematical modeling in areas such as operations research, machine learning, and optimization to plan, design, and operate supply chain systems. The main areas modeled are logistics, production, and pricing. This is a career that requires advanced knowledge of math and draws from several different types of engineering, including industrial, manufacturing, systems, information, and software engineering.

Like other industrial engineers, supply chain engineers may work in offices or in the field. Since most of their work involves computers, most of their work will be in an office environment.

Qualities

Good qualities for a supply chain engineer include the following:

- Math skills
- Communication skills
- Critical-thinking skills
- Creativity
- Problem-solving skills
- People skills
- Computer/technology skills

Working Conditions

Supply chain engineers generally work full time. Hours may vary, depending on the project. Supply chain engineers work as part of a team that gathers information, analyzes data, and identifies solutions.

Job Outlook

The BLS includes supply chain engineers in the larger category of industrial engineers. They predict that employment opportunities will grow 10 percent by 2029, which is faster than the average for all occupations.[12] This is partly because industrial engineering is a versatile job that is needed in many industries.

Other Supply Chain Careers

There are many different titles within the world of ground transportation and supply chain management. Some are entry level, and some are more managerial. Some have a path to advancement, and others might be welcome to an experienced driver who's ready to get off the road. Here's a quick snapshot of just a few of the other related careers you might want to consider.

Entry-Level Supply Chain Jobs

Inventory Clerk
- Maintains records of goods or materials stored in a warehouse or distribution center, including receiving and counting items as they come in.
- Compares inventory records to actual goods present.
- Labels stock with company-approved labels or tags.
- Average annual salary for an inventory clerk is about $36,000.[13]

Production Clerk
- Organizes and expedites workflow.
- Develops and maintains production schedules.
- Develops and distributes work orders within the company departments.
- Expedites delivery/distribution to move materials more quickly.
- Annual salary for production clerks starts at about $53,000.[14]

Supply Chain/Logistics Coordinator
- Coordinates domestic and international shipment order flows.
- Operates the company's warehouse management system (WMS).
- Oversees scheduling, documentation, and staging of imports and exports.

- Maintains communication with carriers, brokers, and freight forwarders.
- Median salary for entry-level supply chain/logistics coordinators is about $36,000.[15]

Mid-level Management Supply Chain Jobs

Operations Manager
- Oversees operations for a private or public company, including coordinating things like production, distribution, and sales.
- Evaluates productivity and looks for potential cost reductions.
- Mostly focused on day-to-day operations within the company itself.
- Helps develop corporate policies and oversee labor.
- Average annual salary about $83,000.[16]

Customer Service Representative
- Works directly with customers to ensure satisfaction, including requests and complaints.
- Monitors accounts.
- Coordinates shipments and deliveries as well as returns and exchanges.
- Average annual salary for supply chain customer service representatives is about $54,000.[17]

Purchasing Agent
- Buys equipment, parts, and services.
- Solicits bids, negotiates and administers contracts, and issues purchase orders.
- Maintains good relationships with suppliers and transportation providers.
- Some of this work is becoming automated and handled by artificial intelligence, but supervision of the machines will be necessary.
- Purchasing agents average about $47,000 in annual salary.[18]

Transportation Specialist
- Oversees and coordinates the safe transport of goods, products, and materials.
- Determines orders to be delivered, and where and when they must arrive.
- Arranges for necessary transportation, including load size; available drivers, carriers, or vehicle fleets; and time frame.
- Average annual salary for a transportation specialist is $50,000.[19]

Supply Chain and Logistics (SCL) Transportation Specialist
- Leads operations for transportation services companies.
- Heads strategic transportation initiatives for wholesale or retail fulfillment operations.
- Chooses carriers, transportation routes, and such to get shipments from the warehouse to the customer.
- Negotiates terms and rates with transportation providers.
- Average annual salary for a supply chain and logistics transportation specialist is about $48,000.[20]

Summary

Ground transportation is an important field at every level. You could be behind the wheel delivering goods around town or across the country or in front of your computer screen planning how those goods will move in the most efficient way. When you become part of America's ground transportation force, you become a vital player in our nation's economy and the well-being of its citizens.

So where do you start? The next chapter is all about planning.

BRIAN BRAGDON, GENERAL TRANSPORTATION MANAGER

Brian Bragdon. *Courtesy of Brian Bragdon*

Brian Bragdon is general transportation manager for the Walmart Supply Chain in Midway, Tennessee. Following his service in the U.S. Army, he earned a bachelor of science degree in industrial engineering from the University of Tennessee, Knoxville. He has many years of experience working in the logistics and supply chain industry. He is skilled in management, customer service, engineering, transportation, and supply chain management.

How did you become a general transportation manager?

I went through college on an ROTC scholarship. My degree is in industrial engineering from UT Knoxville. My first assignment in the army was in a maintenance unit doing service and repair. That got me into that track. With an industrial engineering degree, you could end up on many different career paths. When I left the military, I went through a placement agency and interviewed with a bunch of different companies, including Walmart. I started as a fleet maintenance manager back in 1990, basically responsible for the maintenance organization that repaired Walmart's tractors and trailers. Not being a mechanic, I moved into the operations side, which would be the position level under my current position. That led me to more advancement and being a general transportation manager. I'm now the highest manager at a distribution center for transportation. I moved around the country a lot. I started in Seymour, Indiana, in a new facility in 1990. Then I moved from fleet maintenance to operations in Seymour. Then I went to New Braunfels, Texas, as an operations manager, then Coleman, Alabama, also as an operations manager. Then in May 1995, I went to Woodland, Pennsylvania, as general transportation manager. I'm in my hometown now. I came to Midway, Tennessee, as general transportation manager for the startup of the Midway facility in April 1997. I've had the opportunity to go up to the next level as a regional manager, but I don't want to leave my hometown.

What is a typical day on your job?

One of the exciting things about my role is that there is no typical day. At my level, I'm more mid- and long-range strategic planning, so I work on things like budget, manpower, equipment, what we need six months down the road. The more exciting part is interacting with the 250 or so associates who fall under me, helping them through their day, whether it's work related or personal related. Normally, there are certain key metric reports I look at every morning to see our performance from the previous day, like miles per tractor, safety performance, and so on, to get a pulse for our success. So it's both metrically oriented and taking-care-of-people oriented.

What's the best part of your job?

I would say the best part is that interaction with and helping associates with their challenges, and helping them be successful. My role is like being a football coach or a gymnastics coach—helping people accomplish more than they would on their own. The average age of my associates is fifty-eight or fifty-nine, so I'm dealing with a mature audience. Drivers are gone from their families all week, so I help them deal with that. The people side is the best side.

What's the most challenging part of your job?

The most challenging would be probably the pace that we move forward within Walmart. I've seen a lot of change, a lot of growth. All of the automation and technology that we have that, as an older person, is hard to keep up with—more so for me than for a younger person. I've seen what was a manual day-to-day process become an almost totally automated process, with onboard computers and automated logging systems. What was challenging for me was keeping up with and ahead of all of the technology. When you're the general manager, everyone expects you to have all the answers, and the reality is that I don't have all the answers.

What's the most surprising thing about your job?

The most surprising thing over my career has been to be a part of the growth of this company that started in 1962 with one store and one man's dream and vision, to go to the complexity of Walmart now and the size and scope as a retailer, and the things we do for our customer and our country to help. When I started in 1990, we had just over a thousand truck drivers and 180,000 associates in the company. Now we have ten thousand drivers and 1.8 million associates in the United States and other countries as well. The challenging and exciting part is experiencing that rapid growth, being a part of that.

How did (or didn't) your education prepare you for this job?

I would say that my education prepared me for this job in multiple ways. The ROTC, military science, and my military experience. I'm not saying everyone needs to be in the military, but it helped me develop a set of skills in terms of leadership, initiative, dedication. Transportation is not an eight-to-five job like some industries, it's a twenty-four-hour, 365-days-a-year operation. I tell people that my career sometimes seems like one long day instead of multiple weeks and multiple years! My engineering degree helps with the operational side, the informational systems side. It somewhat prepared me for the skill set you need to have managing an operation. As an engineer, your job is to make things more efficient, to take the waste out, get your people to work smarter, not harder. That applies every day in transportation to what our mission and our goal is.

Is being a general transportation manager what you expected?

It is everything and more than what I expected it to be. The higher up I moved, I've learned the more important it is assisting and helping, taking care of your people. They're your most important asset. As I've moved up, I've focused less on the nuts and bolts because I have a team of managers who do that, and I focus more on the people aspect. It's an exciting career. I've often referred to it as controlled chaos. Transportation is complex and changing. It's not where I thought I'd end up—I thought I'd be in manufacturing, but it was in transportation and it has been exciting.

What's next for you? Where do you see yourself going from here?

In my younger years, I had the desire to move up to the regional level. But the difference is that when you go to the next level, it's more like a staff position. I've always enjoyed being in the trenches with my associates, to help us all have the greatest success that we can get to. The mission is never finished; you can always improve. We don't celebrate the green at Walmart, we celebrate the red—always looking for something you can improve on.

Where do you see the field of distribution management and the supply chain going in the future?

I believe that supply chain/logistics/transportation is among the most, if not the most, evolving career fields out there right now, the most changing and the most challenging for the future. I think it's more challenging and more exciting than it ever has been. COVID-19 has entirely changed the way we think as individuals, how we shop as consumers, and has led to many shifts with the consumer, like home delivery and online groceries. As those services are offered, we have to figure out how to reduce our expenses in transportation, because it doesn't get any cheaper. The consumer drives that—they want what they want when they want it, and they want it fast. Everything that anyone purchases everywhere in the world has to be delivered to somebody, somehow, through transportation. Who knows what the future holds? Drones dropping things in your front yard—who knows? I think transportation is exciting and wide open. The flip side is that it's also scary because a large percentage of everything that moves in this country is moved on a tractor and trailer. There is a driver shortage. So we've got to evolve to other methods of getting from point A to point B.

What is your advice for someone considering this career?

It's a great field; it's a challenging field. You've got to be dedicated to it, you've got to love it, but it's rewarding if you do. From an education standpoint, it's important to have a mix of people-oriented classes and organizational management or supply chain classes. I think, in general, no matter what field you go into, people skills are important. We never know, really, when we're younger where life is going to take us. When I got out of the military with an engineering degree, it didn't seem to make sense to go work for what was then this small retailer. But the more I interacted with the people at Walmart who were interviewing me, the more excited I got about it. Looking back on it thirty years later, I've been blessed. I couldn't have had a more exciting career, to be a part of developing and mentoring so many younger managers. I've had people mentor me, and now I get to be a part of that growth for other people. I really enjoy seeing the success of people who call back to me and say, "I remember when I worked for you!" And working for a national and international company, you get to meet people from all over. I tell people I've worked for two Sams: Uncle Sam in the army and Sam Walton.

Forming a Career Plan

What's So Important about Planning?

Some people know what they want to do from their earliest years, and also seem to know what to do next to reach their goals. But if you're like most people, you can see at least a few different options for your future. And you may be wondering how to make any of those goals a reality.

Taking some time to consider the different career options out there, as well as your own characteristics—what you do best, what you like best, what you don't like at all—can help you narrow down those many options to just the ones that interest you most.

And it's not just important for your first job—it's important to plan ahead so your first job can lead to the next one and the next one, on up the career ladder. When you first get out of school, you may just be focused on finding a job that will pay for your daily, monthly, and yearly living expenses—an apartment, a car, and the things you like to do for fun. And that's fine for a while. But it won't be long before you realize that there's more to life than that. What about all those expenses you have that you didn't really think about earlier (like insurance of all kinds)? What about having a family and home of your own? What about vacations? What about retirement? The earlier you start planning for your future, the better prepared you will be for it when it suddenly becomes the present.

Planning the Plan

In the previous chapter, you got an introduction to the different career options in the field of ground transportation—who does what, what kind of working conditions apply to each type of job, what education and training is required,

It's easier to reach your goals when you know what they are. *Rost-9D/iStock/Getty Images*

and what salary and opportunities are expected for each one. What do you think so far? Does one type of ground transportation job appeal to you more than another?

So What Goes into Your Plan?

In order to plan your plan, you first need to think about yourself. What do you like and dislike? What are you good at and not so good at? What feels like a comfortable fit for you? Next, you'll need to look at the different types of ground transportation jobs and look for the overlap between you and your interests and what the job is actually like.

Another important part of planning is to understand what you can do in advance to get ready to apply for the job you want. How do you become qualified to work in the ground transportation career that appeals to you? What kind of education will you need? What kind of training will you need? And how do you go about getting it?

In this chapter, you'll learn where to start and where to go from there. Let's start by making a few lists.

What Are You Like?

Every good career plan begins with you. A good place to start is by thinking about your own qualities. What are you like? Where do you feel comfortable, and where do you feel uncomfortable? Ask yourself the questions in the sidebar called "All about You" and then think about how your answers match up with a career in ground transportation.

Think about what you're like and what you like to do. *CarlosDavid.org/iStock/Getty Images*

ALL ABOUT YOU

PERSONALITY TRAITS

- Are you introverted or extroverted?
- How do you react to stress? Do you stay calm when others panic?
- Are you good with technology and machinery?
- Are you good at explaining or describing things (like giving directions)?
- How much money do you want to make—just enough or all of it?
- What does the word *success* mean to you?

INTERESTS

- Are you interested in seeing different sights every day?
- Are you interested in complex systems?
- Are you interested in helping people?
- Do you like to travel, or do you want to be able to come home every night?
- Are you interested in moving up a clear career ladder?
- Or would you like to move around from one kind of job to another?

LIKES AND DISLIKES

- Do you like to figure things out or to know ahead of time exactly what's coming up?
- Do you like working on your own or as part of a team?
- Do you like talking to people, or do you prefer minimal interaction?
- Do you like computers?
- Do you like to drive?
- Are you comfortable in small, enclosed spaces?
- Do you like to be outdoors or indoors?
- Do you like to figure out problems and solve them?
- Can you take direction from a boss or teacher, or do you want to decide for yourself how to do things?
- Do you like things to be predictable or to change a lot?

STRENGTHS AND CHALLENGES

- What is something you did that you're proud of?
- Are you naturally good at school, or do you have to work harder at some subjects?
- Are you physically strong and active or not so much?
- Are you flexible and able to adapt to changes and new situations?
- What is your best trait (in your opinion)?
- What is your worst trait (in your opinion)?

Remember, this list is for only you. You're not trying to impress anyone or tell anyone what you think they want to hear. You're just talking to *you*. Be as honest as you can—tell yourself the truth, not what you think someone else would want the answer to be. Once you've got a good list about your own interests, strengths, challenges, likes, and dislikes, you'll be in a good position to know what kind of career you want.

What Are the Jobs Like?

Now it's time to think about the characteristics of the different possible jobs you might do. Take a look at the questions in the sidebar called "About the Job" and consider the similarities and differences between different ground transportation jobs.

ABOUT THE JOB

- What kind of work will you be doing?
- What kind of environment will you be working in?
- Will you have regular nine-to-five hours or evenings, weekends, and overtime?
- Will you travel away from home for extended periods?
- What kind of community would you be living in—city, suburb, or small town?

- Will you be able to live where you want to? Or will you need to go where the job is?
- Will you work directly with customers?
- What will your coworkers be like?
- How much education and training will you need?
- Do you need certification or a special license?
- Is there room for advancement?
- What does the job pay?
- What kind of benefits will the job provide (if any)?
- Will you join a union?
- Is there room to change jobs and try different things?

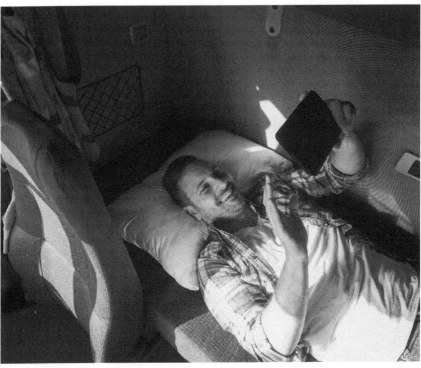

What will your work environment be like? *Smederevac/iStock/Getty Images*

Where to Learn More

There is so much information on the internet—about jobs and everything else—that it can be hard to separate the good data from the noise. So let's take a look at how to find good information about careers in ground transportation.

Start Where You Are

If you're in high school, you can start with your guidance counselor. A guidance counselor's job includes talking to you about your plans beyond graduation and helping you make plans and decisions. If you're working on a GED at a community college or somewhere similar, make an appointment at the career office or just walk in the door. Be sure to tell the counselor what you are interested in doing. *Speak up!* Remember, your counselor can't read your mind—tell them what you're thinking so they can give you appropriate advice. And don't stop there!

Talk to the Pros

Are there ground transportation companies in your area? That could be anything from a local moving and storage company to a trucking company, to a transportation hub for a large corporation, to a local or national delivery service, or to a local transit authority, charter bus company, or taxi or limousine service.

Give them a call and see if someone will give you a tour of the facility or an informational interview about what it's like to work there. Ask for advice on where to train or what kind of college degrees to consider.

Look It Up

Do some research! Check out books from the library and visit websites for the businesses and organizations in your area, as well as larger ground transportation companies. Some have sites all over the world. And don't forget to see the "Further Resources" section at the end of this book.

What Do Employers Want?

So what else do employers look for? There are certain qualities that make someone a valuable employee no matter what job they do.

KNOW YOUR STUFF

The first thing employers want is for you to have all the necessary qualifications for the job. When you read chapter 1, you got an idea of the kind of qualifications you need for different jobs in ground transportation. For some, you need a commercial driver's license (CDL), and for others you need a bachelor's or master's degree. Part of your plan is to make sure that you are building the credentials that match the job you want to do. For instance, if you want to be a long-haul trucker, it doesn't really matter if you have an MBA degree, but you have to have that Class A CDL.

Good people skills are essential to any job. *kali9/E+/Getty Images*

GOOD PEOPLE SKILLS

The ability to get along with people is one of the most important factors of a successful career in any field. Good people skills can be summed up as treating others the way you would want them to treat you. The following is a comprehensive list of good people skills:

- Be understanding and respectful toward other people.
- Be patient—no one is perfect (including you).
- Pay attention and show genuine interest—everyone has something interesting about them. Take the time to find out what it is.
- Try to see the other person's point of view (even if it's different from yours).
- Empathy and compassion go a long way.

Some of the most important people skills you can have are being able to communicate clearly and effectively and having good character.

COMMUNICATION SKILLS

Good communication is essential in work and in life. Basic communication skills include the following:

- **Active listening:** Pay attention to what the other person is actually saying and respond to it. Don't just plan what you're going to say next.
- **Speaking:** Express yourself simply and clearly in spoken words.
- **Writing:** Express yourself simply, clearly, and with sufficient detail in writing. Avoid a lot of extra words that can confuse the reader, but don't leave out anything important.
- **Body language:** Nonverbal communication is just as important as verbal communication. Pay attention to the messages you're sending with your face, gestures, and posture, and pay attention to the nonverbal messages you're receiving from the people around you.

CHARACTER

Your character includes your personality and the choices you make based on your values and beliefs. Important character traits include the following:

- **Honesty and trust:** Honesty and trust form the basis of any relationship, whether personal or professional. This includes trusting others as well as being trustworthy yourself. When you and your coworkers know you can count on each other, you can accomplish anything. And when customers know they can trust you and the work you do for them, you will be set up for a lifetime of success.
- **A sense of humor:** Knowing when to use humor to lighten a situation is a great people skill. Used appropriately, humor can diffuse tension and conflict. It's good to be able and willing to laugh at yourself. But be careful—using humor to mock or belittle others is not funny and has no place on the job.
- **Being supportive and helpful:** Offer to do a little more than required or to help someone out when they need it. If someone is having a hard day, be respectful of their feelings.
- **Flexibility:** Be ready to adapt to changing situations, conditions, and workflow.
- **Good judgment:** Choose your own behavior—don't just go along with something if your gut says it's not a good idea.

When you get to chapter 4, you'll learn more about putting your people skills into action to get and keep the job you want.

BE A HARD WORKER

This one might seem obvious, but it's so important that it's worth spelling it out. Every employer wants employees who are willing to put in the effort to get the job done—and not just done, but done efficiently and well. When you work hard for a fair employer, the company will prosper, and you will prosper with it. (If you work hard and don't prosper along with the company, you should probably start looking for another job.)

You can start demonstrating that you're a hard worker while you're still in high school (see the section titled "Making School Count" later in the chapter). A reputation as a hard worker in school or with previous employers will naturally turn into good recommendations down the line when you're applying for a job.

MAKE YOUR BED EVERY DAY

Why should you make your bed every day? It's about developing habits—the kind of habits that will make you successful at whatever job you turn your hand to.

One of the most important habits you can build is finishing what you start (or "task completion"). If you already have this habit mastered, good for you! You've already got one of the keys to long-term success. But if you don't, you can practice and build that habit by simply deciding to make your bed every day. Then doing it.

Retired U.S. Navy Admiral Seal William H. McCraven wrote an entire book[1] about it. In a speech, he explained,

> If you make your bed every morning, you will have accomplished the first task of the day. It will give you a small sense of pride, and it will encourage you to do another task, and another, and another. And by the end of the day that one task completed will have turned into many tasks completed.[2]

Author Brian Tracy said,

> Disciplining yourself to concentrate on a job until it is finished gives you a feeling of confidence, competence, and mastery. It develops you into a hard-working person and gives you an experience of self-control, so you feel that you are in charge of your own destiny.[3]

So go ahead—give it a try! Start by making your bed every day for a week. Then do another week. Then a month. Soon it's a habit. Your space is neater, you sleep better, and most important, you're on your way to being someone who finishes what they start.

Planning for the Job You Want

Now you've learned a bit about yourself and about what employers will want from you. You've started to think about the qualities you're looking for in your future career. So now let's take a look at how that might look when you compare who you are to the jobs that exist in ground transportation.

If you . . .

- are extroverted
- stay calm under stress
- are good with machinery
- are good at describing places and things
- like to see different sights and meet different people
- like to work on your own
- want a regular schedule where you can be home every night but also have some variety

. . . then you might like driving a taxicab.

If you . . .

- want to make good money
- want to travel
- don't mind enclosed spaces
- are physically strong and have good vision and hearing
- don't mind long hours
- can follow rules and legal requirements
- can stay alert and have the sense to rest when you need to

. . . then you might like being a long-haul truck driver.

If you . . .

- are interested in complex systems and how things work
- are good at math and computers
- want to work regular hours
- want to usually come home at night but don't mind some travel
- can interact well with different kinds of people at every level of a business
- intend to go to college
- are interested in being promoted up the career ladder

. . . then you might want to be a logistician, distribution manager, or supply chain engineer.

You get the idea. Try out several options and see what you think!

Comparing Different Job Options

To plan your future, it's good to compare what different jobs have to offer. Let's compare some of the careers we looked at in chapter 1 and see what they have in common and what's different in the areas of education/training, license or certification, and compensation.

TAXI DRIVER

Education/Training

There are no formal education requirements to be a taxi driver. Most taxi companies provide a short training period, depending on the company and where they're located, as different cities have different legal requirements for training.

License

At minimum, a taxi driver must have a valid regular driver's license (operator's license). Most towns and cities also require cab drivers to have a taxi or limousine license, which generally includes passing a background check, a drug test, and a written exam about regulations and local geography.

Pay

Taxicabs use a meter to calculate the cost of the ride. The metering system ensures that the amount you earn depends on the number of passenger trips you make. It's customary for the passenger to also tip the cabbie, either in cash or as an add-on to their credit card charge. Cabbies who provide good service and are pleasant to their customers are likely to earn more in tips. Taxi drivers earn an average of about $26,000, including tips. This is about 70 percent of what other types of motor vehicle operators earn and about 67 percent of the U.S. Bureau of Labor Statistics' (BLS) average for all occupations.[4]

CHAUFFEUR

Education/Training

There are no formal education requirements to be a chauffeur or limousine driver, but most have at least a high school diploma. Most limousine companies provide a short training period, depending on the company and where they're located, as different cities have different legal requirements for training.

License/Certification

At minimum, a chauffeur must have a valid regular driver's license (operator's license). Most towns and cities also require cab drivers to have a limousine license, which generally includes passing a background check, a drug test, and a written exam about regulations and local geography. The Federal Motor Carrier Safety Administration (FMCA) requires limousine drivers who will transport sixteen or more passengers (including the driver) at a time to have a commercial driver's license (CDL) with a passenger (P) endorsement. See the sidebar titled "Commercial Driver's Licenses" in chapter 1.

Pay

Like taxi drivers, chauffeurs earn about $26,000 a year, including tips.[5] The highest 10 percent of chauffeurs earn more than $37,000. There are differences in pay rates by state for chauffeurs, with those in California averaging only $25,500, while in Washington, DC, the average is closer to $30,700.

RIDE-HAILING DRIVER

Education/Training

All kinds of people become ride-hailing drivers, from former truckers to artists to college professors. There are no formal education requirements, but individual companies will have their own requirements for training, employment history, background checks, and the like.

License

Ride-hailing drivers need a regular, valid operator's license. Other regulations vary by state or city, as well as by the ride-hailing company you drive for. For instance, both Uber and Lyft require that, in addition to your license, you have at least a year of driving experience and that you use a four-door vehicle that meets their specifications, along with proof of residency and proof of insurance. They also do a driving record and criminal background check. You need a working cell phone that will run their app; the company websites have information about recommendations and settings for software.

Pay

Because so many ride-hailing drivers make their own hours or work part time to supplement other jobs, it's hard to find annual salary figures. Some information is available, although things vary by state and by company. In 2018, for instance, Uber drivers made about $24.77 per hour in fares. However, $8.33 of that went back to the company in commissions and fees. The driver is responsible for gas, insurance, and maintenance on their vehicle. Once self-employment taxes and health insurance are paid for, the driver is left with an hourly income that's close to minimum wage.[6]

BUS DRIVER

Education/Training

Most employers expect bus drivers to have a high school diploma or GED. Training includes practicing maneuvering the bus on a closed course, then driving in light traffic, and moving up to the kind of route you'll be driving. New drivers generally are accompanied by an experienced driver for a period of time. There is also in-class training where you cover the company's rules and regulations, state and municipal traffic laws, safe driving practices, schedules and bus routes, fares, and how to interact with passengers.

License

Generally, all bus drivers need a CDL with a (P) endorsement (see the sidebar titled "Commercial Driver's Licenses" in chapter 1). School bus drivers need the (S) endorsement on their CDL. You can earn your CDL on the job; if you already have a CDL, your training may be shorter. Many states require that bus drivers be at least twenty-one years old. Your license can be revoked or suspended if you've had a CDL suspended in another state, if you've been convicted of a felony involving the use of a motor vehicle or of driving under the influence of alcohol or drugs. The FMCSA maintains a list of other potential violations.

Pay

Compensation varies by what kind of bus you drive, where you go, and how long you're away from home.[7] The following is a list of annual wages for different types of bus drivers:

- **School Bus Driver:** The median annual wage for school bus drivers is about $32,400, which is 77 percent of what transit and intercity bus drivers make. This is partly because school bus drivers essentially work less than full time since school buses are usually only needed at the beginning and end of the school day, during the school year. Some school bus drivers supplement their income by holding other staff jobs in the schools, like working in the cafeteria or as a mechanic or janitor. Also, some school buses are used for camps and summer programs, which can provide additional work when school is out.
- **Local Transit Bus Driver:** The median annual wage for local transit bus drivers was more than $42,000.
- **Intercity Bus Driver:** The median annual wage for intercity bus drivers was more than $42,000. The lowest 10 percent earned less than $25,550, and the highest 10 percent earned more than $69,070.
- **Charter Bus Driver:** According to the BLS, charter bus drivers earn a median annual wage of about $31,440.

PARATRANSIT VAN DRIVER

License and Pay

Requirements for paratransit van drivers vary considerably by state and by company. Some require a CDL, but others don't. For instance, a recent job listing for a regional transit authority in a Massachusetts city did not require a CDL and paid between $26,000 and $37,000 annually. Another listing was for a mobility company in Colorado, which also did not require a CDL, paid $17 an hour plus benefits for part-time workers, and required an age of at least twenty-one, a high school diploma, a good driving record, and random drug and motor vehicle checks.

SHORT-HAUL TRUCKING: LOCAL DELIVERY DRIVER

Education/Training

Most delivery truck drivers have a high school diploma or equivalent (e.g., GED). Many companies train their drivers on the job, under the supervision of an experienced driver. At the same time, drivers learn their company's policies about drop-offs, returns, payments, and dealing with damaged goods. At some large companies, a warehouse employee can learn to be a driver and move into that role.

License

To drive most delivery trucks, dump trucks, or large straight trucks, you'll need at least a Class B CDL. If you might be transporting hazardous materials, you'll also need the (H) endorsement.

Pay

The BLS reports a median annual wage for light truck drivers as $34,730 per year, with those working as courier/messengers making closer to $49,000 and those in retail and wholesale trade averaging between $26,000 and $33,400 annually.

SHORT-HAUL TRUCKING: REGIONAL DRIVER

Education/Training

Most companies expect truck drivers to have a high school diploma or equivalent (e.g., GED). Professional truck driving schools teach courses that cover how to maneuver large vehicles in traffic on highways or crowded streets. These classes also cover the federal laws and regulations on interstate truck driving. Programs at private truck-driving schools or at a community college usually last three to six months. Drivers receive a certificate to show they've completed the course. You can expect several weeks of on-the-job training, as well, with an experienced driver/mentor. This gives you a chance to get familiar with the truck you'll be driving, learn the route and how to handle the cargos you'll be carrying, and master the company's specific rules and regulations.

License

Regional truck drivers need a CDL (see the sidebar in chapter 1 titled "Commercial Driver's Licenses") that corresponds to the kind of truck they'll be driving. Usually that's a Class A license, which covers everything up to tractor-trailers, truck and trailer combinations, tanker vehicles, livestock carriers, or flatbeds. If you're going to be carrying hazardous materials, you'll need to get the (H) endorsement and pass a background check.

Pay

According to ZipRecruiter, regional truck drivers averaged about $61,000 per year in 2021 (around $29 per hour). That salary can vary a lot by location. For instance, New York City (which has a very active job market for regional truck drivers) averages closer to $71,160 per year.[8] Bear in mind that higher-paying cities may also have higher costs of living. While regional truck drivers make less money than long-haul truck drivers, they report much greater job satisfaction and rank that satisfaction more highly than the dollar figure.[9]

LONG-HAUL TRUCK DRIVER

Education/Training

Education requirements for long-haul truckers are basically the same as for regional truck drivers. Most companies expect truck drivers to have a high school diploma or equivalent (e.g., GED). Professional truck driving schools teach courses that cover how to maneuver large vehicles in traffic on highways or crowded streets. These classes also cover the federal laws and regulations on interstate truck driving. Programs at private truck-driving schools or at a community college usually last three to six months. Drivers receive a certificate to show they've completed the course. On-the-job training with an experienced driver/mentor helps new drivers get familiar with the equipment, how to handle the cargos you'll be carrying, the routes, federal rules and regulations, and the company's own policies.

License

Long-haul truckers need a Class A CDL with any and all appropriate endorsements for the cargo you'll be carrying. See the sidebar titled "Commercial Driver's Licenses" in chapter 1, and check with your state Department of Motor Vehicles (DMV). Remember that to keep your CDL, you will have to maintain a clean driving record and pass the Department of Transportation (DOT) physical every two years. Expect random drug and alcohol tests, and know that your CDL can be suspended for a variety of reasons. Some employers have even stricter standards than the FMCSA—be sure you know what is expected of you. It's always better to be too safe than not safe enough.

Pay

The BLS reports the median annual wage for heavy and tractor-trailer truck drivers as $45,260 in May 2019, with the top 10 percent earning at least $66,800.[10] Some companies report much higher salaries, with different segments of the wage paid at different per mile rates for mileage, performance,

HazMat, and annual increases. This will vary by employer and by demand for drivers (see the sidebar titled "Truckers Needed!" in chapter 1). Long-haul truckers who own their own vehicle (owner-operators) are generally paid a percentage of the revenue from shipping.

There are ground transportation and supply chain jobs at every level. *gorodenkoff/iStock/Getty Images*

DISTRIBUTION/SUPPLY CHAIN MANAGER (LOGISTICIAN)

Education/Training

Most companies hiring distribution managers/logisticians look for someone with a bachelor's degree in a field like business administration, economics, management, manufacturing, statistics, systems engineering, or supply chain management. Ideally, that should include coursework in operations and database management as well as system dynamics. Most programs also offer courses covering software and technologies commonly used by logisticians, such as radio-frequency identification (RFID). Many people in these positions hold master's degrees (such as an MBA) as well. It will be important to develop skills in cost accounting, project management, global awareness, business ethics, and e-business/e-procurement systems.

Previous work experience in a related field can be beneficial, and these roles are often filled by someone who already works for the company in another job like inventory control analyst, warehouse supervisor, or traffic manager. Experience could also come from working in a logistical support role, like a dispatcher or clerk, or from experience gained during military service.

Certification

There is no specific certification required for distribution managers or logisticians, but several professional organizations offer certifications that show you know what you're doing. Professional certifications for supply chain management include the following:

- CPSM (Certified Professional in Supply Management®) is a globally recognized credential from the Institute for Supply Management (ISM) that demonstrates competence in sixteen important areas.
- CPIM (certified in production and inventory management) demonstrates deep understanding of forecasting, master scheduling, materials management, production planning, and the extended supply chain.
- CSCP (certified supply chain professional) shows that you understand the essential concepts, strategies, and technology affecting the extended supply chain.

If you plan to work for the U.S. Department of Defense (DOD), you'll need to earn specific certifications to qualify. Check out the "Further Resources" section at the end of the book to learn more about professional organizations and what they offer.

Pay

According to the BLS (which reports this career under the title of "Logistician"), the median annual salary was $74,750 as of May 2019. The highest 10 percent earned more than $120,400.[11] As of 2021, Glassdoor reported the average annual salary for a supply chain manager was $61,915, with the low end at about $44,000 and the high end at about $85,000. It's common for supply chain managers to receive bonuses in addition to their salaries; an average annual bonus is about $99,000, and top performers receive much more.[12]

SUPPLY CHAIN ENGINEER

Education/Training

Supply chain engineers typically begin with a bachelor's degree, usually a bachelor of science (BS) in industrial engineering or another engineering field. These degree programs balance classroom learning with hands-on labs. Supply chain engineers will need to know higher-level mathematics (algebra, trigonometry, and calculus), computer science, and newer technologies like blockchain, artificial intelligence, and more. Some supply chain engineers also hold master's degrees. This is helpful if you plan to become a technical specialist and/or supervise teams of engineers and technicians. To teach at the college or university level, you'd need to go on for a doctoral degree.

License/Certification

Supply chain engineers don't need a license for entry-level jobs. As you look to move up in your career, a professional engineering (PE) license issued by your state can be acquired later in your career. The PE lets you move into higher levels of leadership and independence, oversee the work of other engineers, sign off on projects, and provide services directly to the public. To earn a PE, you must have the following:

- A degree from an ABET-accredited engineering program
- A passing score on the Fundamentals of Engineering (FE) exam
- Relevant work experience, typically at least four years
- A passing score on the professional engineering (PE) exam[13]

Depending on your state, you may have to pass other intermediate tests and maintain your license with continuing education.

Pay

According to the BLS (which includes this career under the category "industrial engineers"), the median annual wage as of May 2019 was $88,020. The lowest

10 percent earned under $57,000 and the highest 10 percent earned more than $134,000.[14]

Making School Count

Once you know what you want to do, you'll need to plan how to learn to do that job. We'll go into detail on that in chapter 3, "Pursuing the Education Path." But what about now—while you're in high school? How can you get the most out of your high school education if you want to have a career in ground transportation?

GRADUATE

The most important thing that you can do to make your high school education count, of course, is to *graduate*. There are people who believe that finishing high school isn't all that important if you're going into a hands-on job like being a commercial driver or working in a warehouse. Perhaps you know some older people—even relatives—who went into a job before finishing high school. Maybe they're telling you that you can or should do that, too. This might have been a valid career path in some places a long time ago, but it isn't now.

In some states, you might be able to earn a CDL without a high school diploma or GED, but it's not usual. Most employers list a high school diploma or GED as the first requirement on job postings, even if they intend to train you. That's because a high school diploma or GED shows that you can take on some responsibility and finish what you start. And if you want to go into a job (or be promoted into one) that needs a college degree, you'll have to have a high school diploma or GED to move forward.

Most important, everything you learn in high school will come in handy on the job and in life—math, English, computers, and business classes most of all. Don't forget driver's education! If you've already left high school without graduating, get your GED as soon as you can.

WHAT CLASSES SHOULD YOU TAKE?

Take the full range of general education courses in high school. Math, English, communications, and business classes are all useful choices. If you're interested in supply chain management, you'll want to take higher-level math, computers, statistics, and data analysis, if those classes are available. If your high school offers trades or vocational courses, especially anything to do with mechanics, auto repair, or computers, take those classes!

Make the effort to study hard and do as well as you can in every class. You're learning more than just the subject matter. You're learning how to learn, and how to tackle a project and see it through to the end. And *that* is a priceless skill that you can learn for free in high school.

Summary

Now you know how to plan your plan! Everything you need to know is easily available to you. You just need to put out your hand and pick it up.

Your plan will contain the following:

- Insight into who you are and what you're good at (as well as what you'd like to avoid)
- What you want out of your career in ground transportation
- What the different kinds of ground transportation jobs are like
- What kind of education and experience you need to achieve your goals
- Ideas to improve or hone your people skills

Don't miss the "Further Resources" section at the end of the book. You'll find plenty of additional sources to help you figure out your plan.

In the next chapter, "Pursuing the Education Path," we'll look at what kinds of educational options are available, and we'll answer the most important question—how do you pay for it? Don't worry! It's easier than you might think.

JASON GRAY, TRUCK DRIVER

Jason Gray (left) with New Hampshire governor Chris Sununu and Eric Miller (see Eric's interview in chapter 4). *Photo by Vera Tucker/NH Motor Transit Association*

Jason Gray is a truck driver with a Class B CDL. As an independent contractor, he works with RJ Crowley Moving & Storage in central New Hampshire (see the interview with Eric Miller in chapter 4) driving a straight truck (that's a box truck, not a semi). He's been in the business for more than forty years, including about twenty-five years with Crowley's. In 2019, he was awarded the New Hampshire Motor Transport Association's Master Truck Driver Certification, a prestigious award to recognize professional vehicle operators who have made a career of driving large vehicles and who have contributed to the community and the safety of the driving public through their character, experience, and good judgment.

How did you decide to become a truck driver?

I didn't really decide to; it just happened. My stepfather was a tractor-trailer truck driver on a Boston–Connecticut–New York route. When I was eighteen, I didn't really know what I was going to do. I met Bob Crowley [late owner of RJ Crowley Moving & Storage], and he gave me a job as a mover. Then I wanted to make more money, so I started driving. Bob was like a second father to me. He always made sure I had a job and had an income. He was someone I looked up to.

What is a typical trip on your job?

It can vary, but I could travel from Maine to Key West. I've been out West many times, but now I pretty much stay on the East Coast, the whole Eastern Seaboard. If I were going from here to Orlando, for instance, I'd leave my house at two in the morning. You're only allowed eleven hours of driving time out of a fourteen-hour shift, so the whole point of leaving that early is to get through Boston and New York early in the morning to avoid the traffic. Then you keep going until you meet your maximum hours. (The new regulations say I have to stop for a half hour within the first eight hours, but that counts against my fourteen hours.) How long a route takes depends on traffic—I've sat on the George Washington Bridge for four and a half hours and not moved. That comes out of my drive time, even though I'm not making any progress. When COVID first came out and everyone was restricted for travel, I was headed to Florida and there was nobody on the road. I averaged seventy-five miles per hour all the way there!

As an independent contractor, I'm in charge of everything that happens after I pull out of the lot. I have a crew here that helps me load the trucks. We have to keep the weight balanced, so I'm not overloaded in the front or the back. There are DOT scales that you have to abide by. If you're overweight they shut you down, so you have to find another truck to take the weight off. There are inspection points where they look at your weight, your logbooks or ELD—that's your electronic logging device. If you're off by a little bit, they shut you down for twenty-four hours and you can't leave. You're pretty much driving your own office with deadlines that are almost impossible to reach. When I get to my destination, I have to hire qualified people to help me offload the truck. There are networks of moving companies that help you find moving help in the area, like the Brotherhood and Sisterhood of Moving, and I also work with certain crews I've used before. I can book them in advance, but if something happens where I can't be there on time, I still have to pay them.

What's the best part of your job?

In the moving business, I've met some really outlandish and important people! I've moved NFL players, government employees. The most ironic one was a government prosecutor who moved under a different name. I'd actually gone to high school with him! But I had to keep quiet about who he was and what he did. I've moved a museum. I've moved very expensive cars—I shipped a car that auctioned for more than a million dollars. I put a stuffed cow on Beacon Street in Boston—it was a family pet that they had stuffed. I've moved some weird stuff!

One part I really like about my job: the older people get, the less and less they can do for themselves. When I relocate them, I try to give them every discount I can because moving is very expensive. I like to help elderly people get started on their next stage of life. Oh! And I got to meet the governor because I drove a certain number of miles without an accident. I got an award for 85,000 hours of service. I've been in the business a long time!

What's the most challenging part of your job?

Loading the truck. It's like putting a puzzle together every day. You have to balance, you only have so many cubic feet in the truck, you have to get it in there just the right way, so nothing gets scratched or damaged. It's a knack I have that not everyone has. Putting it all in there the right way is the whole key. The other challenge is trying to maintain a health card. Depending on where you go, sometimes they give you a three-month card if you need to address an issue, or if you're diabetic you get a six-month card. If you pass with good colors you get it for two years.

What's the most surprising thing about your job?

I think the most surprising thing I've noticed, as of late, is the change in how truckers communicate and help each other—or don't. It's been mind boggling that if you drive for one company you're an elite driver, and if you drive for another you're not. There's an assumption that one company only hires new drivers, so if they get into trouble, they don't help them. There's a lot less camaraderie than there used to be. Also, the newer trucks are automatic, so the people just coming out of school get ragged on for driving an automatic truck, when it's not even their choice. I prefer a standard, but I'll take an automatic in the city!

How did (or didn't) your education or training prepare you for your job?

Training? [Laughs.] It was June 5, 1989. Bob Crowley put me in a truck and said "Go"! So I went. My heart was racing! I can remember that day like it was yesterday! It was a split shift. After that, I pretty much taught myself. When I was told I needed a commercial license, I went to the state and took a three-part test. The written test involves driving questions and questions about the truck. After that, you get a learner's permit that allows you to drive in the state with a licensed driver. Then you take a driving test, starting with a pre-trip inspection of the whole vehicle. You go around the whole truck and tell the instructor what you're looking for and why you're looking for it. The instructor pulls out pieces of the truck, and you have to know what the piece is and what it's for. You have to know what the cam is and does, what the air canisters are, how much air you can lose in a minute, what the tread on the tire should be, how to test your parking brake, know your PSIs for the vehicle, that everything is latched and the latches are in working order, and lots of other things. The first time I did my pre-trip, the truck failed inspection—it was about forty years old. We drove it down there and had to have it towed back!

Is your job what you expected it to be?

It was exactly the way I expected it to be. There are so many avenues you can go with this job. The way the business has changed over the years, the state and local agencies that regulate it. For customers, you really have to do your research on who you hire—there are a lot of fly-by-night businesses that open that don't really follow the rules so they have no bills to pay and they charge much less. Then they do half a summer's worth of work and just close their doors and there's nothing the customer can do about it. But we have to be reliable because we're going to be around. Then when the customer calls us to bail them out, we can't help them because we're already booked. But I get to see a lot of great things, meet a lot of great people.

What's next? Where do you see yourself going from here?

I knew where I was going when Bob was still here. Then when the business was sold, I told Eric I'd stay for a year while he learned the business. So last spring the year ended, and he asked me what I was going to do, and I stayed on. I don't know what I'm going to do, but I'm not going to drive a truck again or pick up another piece of furniture. One of the biggest downfalls of driving a truck is that you're just never home. You can be a stranger to your kids. I want to find a cozy desk somewhere!

What is your advice for a young person considering this career?

Research who you work for. Research what you want to haul, your cargo. Flatbeds haul certain materials; tankers haul other things; box trucks haul other things. Research the company; see what their benefits and rates are. Research what you want to be pulling. You don't want to pull for a company that pays you great money to go to California, but they don't have a load for you to return, so you're stuck in California and your money is no good.

A lot of drivers now are taking online courses while they're driving. You have to take the rest time, so you can take online classes and listen to audio classes. That way you can do something else later on. I've been in truck stops where they have school supplies. You might be stuck there for thirty-six hours, but you can be learning. I met a woman in a Savannah, Georgia, truck stop—she was reading a psychology book, and she's going to be a psychologist when she finishes. It'll take a long time, but she's doing it. I don't know that I would choose this again as a career. It might have been better to do it for a while as a life experience and then move on.

Pursuing the Education Path

What Kind of Education Will You Need?

*D*epending on your plans, your educational needs could be very different. For someone interested in driving a truck, you probably won't need a bachelor's degree. But depending on where and how you earn your commercial driver's license (CDL), you may have the opportunity to earn an associate degree alongside your training. On the other hand, if you're looking to go into a managerial role in distribution or supply chain management or logistics, you'll need a bachelor's degree to start—you may even go on for a master's degree.

We've all been hearing a lot about the high cost of college tuition these days, along with questions about whether everyone even needs to go to college. You've looked over the ground transportation jobs in this book and seen that there are some where you can begin with just a high school diploma.

There are education pathways for every part of the ground transportation industry. *jacoblund/iStock/ Getty Images*

For those careers where higher education is essential, it is possible to earn a degree in a cost-effective way—if you do a little research ahead of time. It also helps to understand how financial aid works (see the "What's It Going to Cost You?" section and the sidebar called "Not All Financial Aid Is Created Equal" later in this chapter).

The Training Option

DO YOU NEED A LICENSE?

If you're planning to be a professional driver, you'll first need to qualify. Every state has their own rules, even for very similar jobs, so the first thing you'll need to do is check with the Department of Motor Vehicles (DMV) in your state to find out what's required. It's up to you to know what license you need for the kind of driving you plan to do.

You can earn a CDL through a community college, private trucking school, or even your employer.
Comstock/Stockbyte/Getty Images

Taxi Driver/Chauffeur License

As an example of how different state requirements can be, licensing for taxis and chauffeurs is often regulated at the municipal (town or city) level rather than at the state level. Some are very easy and some are quite complex (like New York City).

Example: Manchester, New Hampshire, Taxi License

A license to drive a taxicab in Manchester, New Hampshire, is issued by the City of Manchester. You need a valid New Hampshire driver's license (not a CDL). Then just complete an application from the Office of the City Clerk and submit it with a current copy of your motor vehicle record and your criminal record (if you have one), certified by the New Hampshire Department of Safety (or the appropriate out-of-state agencies if you've been a resident of any other state in the past five years). You need to provide two recent passport photographs and pay an $80 application fee. The application is generally processed between one day and one week before a taxicab license can be issued. All taxicab driver licenses expire each year on April 30.[1]

The state of New Hampshire does not require any special license for a chauffeur.

Example: New York City Taxi License

To drive a taxi in New York City, you'll need a CDL with the right endorsement. New York has more types of licenses than we covered in chapter 1. They have Class A, Class B, and Class C, but they also have some other licenses that may apply if you want to be a New York cabbie; you have to meet requirements and pay fees to more than one agency.

New York Department of Motor Vehicles
To drive a cab in New York, you need either a Class A, B, or C CDL or a Class E license. To get the Class E license, you have to qualify for the regular Class D operator's license. You need a special application form to upgrade from Class D to Class E.[2]

- **Class D operator's license:** This license is for people aged eighteen or over (or seventeen if you took Driver Education). Class D lets you operate passenger cars and trucks with a gross vehicle weight rating (GVWR) of 26,000 pounds or less; a vehicle that tows another vehicle (like a trailer) with a maximum gross weight of 10,000 pounds or less; or tow a vehicle with a GVWR of 10,000 pounds or more only if the combined weight rating of the two vehicles is 26,000 pounds or less.
- **Class E for-hire taxi, livery, limo license:** This license is for people aged eighteen or older. You can operate the same type of vehicles as Class D, plus for-hire vehicles that carry fourteen passengers or less.
- **New York City Taxi and Limousine Commission (NYCTLC):** Next, you need to get a TLC license from the NYCTLC, which will let you drive a yellow taxi, green taxi (yes, there are different rules for different color cabs), livery, black car, or limousine. If you want to drive a commuter van, paratransit van, or for-hire vehicle, there are different licenses for that. And there are different fees at various stages along the way.

Bus License—Transit

Check with your state's Department of Transportation to see which class of CDL you'll need to drive a bus in your area. Look for a driver training program that offers commercial driver's license training. Don't worry if the program seems tailored to truck drivers. Talk with someone in the program to make sure that what you learn will apply to buses as well as trucks. These programs are usually one to three months longer. You'll need to pass both written and driving tests to obtain a CDL with the passenger (P) endorsement.

Expect to train for six months or so with a licensed bus driver. Whether you work for a municipal transit authority or a charter bus company, you'll be trained on the organization's own equipment, systems, policies, and procedures.

Example: Framingham, Massachusetts

The MetroWest Regional Transit Authority (MWRTA) in Framingham, Massachusetts, runs its own CDL training program financed by the State of Massachusetts.[3]

- **Prerequisite:** Valid Massachusetts driver's license and no felony convictions or DUI/OUI within the last five years.
- **CDL Permit Class:** Two-day-long class to prepare students for both the General Knowledge Exam and the Passenger Endorsement Test. The permit is a prerequisite for the practical class.
- **CDL Practical Class:** Ten to twelve hours of hands-on training consisting of three parts: pre-trip inspection, skills (course), and an on-road portion.
- **CDL Test:** Administered within two weeks of completing the practical class.
- Once the program is completed, the student must take their current license, stamped permit paper, and Medical DOT (Department of Transportation) card and go to a registry to upgrade to a new Class C commercial driver's license with a passenger (P) endorsement. There are various fees along the way.

School Bus License

Depending on your state, you may need a Class A, Class B, or Class C CDL to drive a school bus. What you will need in any state is the very important passenger (P) and school bus (S) endorsements on your CDL. You'll also need to pass background checks and drug screening tests, have a clean driving record, meet vision and hearing requirements, and usually have to be able to speak and read English. You might also need to have some experience working with children.

Example: California

The state of California has many requirements for school bus drivers. To qualify, you must be at least eighteen years old with good moral character, be in good physical condition, and have clean driving and criminal records. You also have to "have the desire and patience to work with children."[4]

To try for your California school bus driver's license, you must do the following:

- Attend a minimum of twenty hours of classroom instruction.
- Pass a physical examination (no epilepsy, type 1 diabetes, or high blood pressure).
- Pass four written tests at the DMV.
- Pass two written tests at the California Highway Patrol (CHP).
- Train a minimum of twenty hours behind the wheel.
- Pass a driving test with the CHP.
- Pass a pre-employment drug test and finger printing for the district that hires you.[5]

Qualified California school bus drivers must also attend at least ten hours of training each year and are randomly tested for drugs and alcohol. There is a long list of convictions and violations that can prevent someone from obtaining a California school bus driver's license, including (but not limited to) reckless driving, driving under the influence, violent crimes, cruelty to spouse or child, making false statements on certificate or endorsement applications, passing bad checks, not passing the health requirements, and lots of others.

Truck License

Truck drivers need a license that matches the equipment they'll be driving. Take another look at the sidebar in chapter 1 titled "Commercial Driver's Licenses." You'll also need to check with your state DMV to see if they have any additional requirements.

Example: Vermont

In the state of Vermont, you can earn a Class A, B, or C CDL or commercial learner's permit (CLP) in accordance with federal standards. The state places restrictions on CDLs that match the vehicle that you took the test in, so be sure to take the test in the type of vehicle you want to qualify for. Vermont has these age requirements:

- You must be at least eighteen years old and hold a valid Vermont Class D driver's license to obtain a CLP.
- You must be at least eighteen years old to obtain a CDL and operate a commercial vehicle within Vermont (intrastate commerce).

- You must be at least twenty-one years old to operate a commercial motor vehicle between Vermont and another state (interstate commerce).[6]

Earn your commercial driver's license. *Smederevac/iStock/Getty Images*

WHERE CAN YOU TRAIN?

To drive any kind of ground transportation vehicle, you first have to be able to drive a car. Taking driver's education while you're still in high school will often mean that you not only have better training and experience but also your insurance rates will be lower. So take driver's education and get your regular driver's license (often called a Class D operator's license).

But then what? It all depends on the vehicle and the state. As we saw earlier in the chapter, this varies a lot by state and by city.

Chauffeur Training

Chauffeurs need more than just a license. In most municipalities, they need to pass tests showing that they can operate the vehicles they will be driving, that they know the city layout and laws, and that they know their vehicles.

They need to learn how to interact with customers who have high expectations for service, safety, discretion, dress, and manners. This is why many limo companies prefer to train their own chauffeurs.

Example: Texas

In the great state of Texas, a limousine (also called vehicle-for-hire) license is different in every city. In addition to the basics (driver's license, clean driving and criminal records, application fee, etc.), there are additional requirements:

- El Paso has appearance standards ("sanitary and well groomed"), and chauffeurs must attend a course on tourist awareness.
- Houston requires a medical history and the name and address of the employer.
- Austin wants applicants to have a ground transportation service company as a primary sponsor and requires passing a chauffeur's test.[7]

Truck and Bus Driver Training

No matter what kind of commercial vehicle you want to drive, you'll need to train for and earn your CDL. You should look for programs that provide classroom instruction as well as behind-the-wheel training. Expect about 160 hours of training (equivalent to four forty-hour weeks). There are several different options:

Community College Certificate Program

Many community colleges offer certificate programs leading to a CDL. These programs usually last four to six weeks, with different tracks for Class A or Class B license seekers. The advantage to community college programs is that the cost is low; additionally, community colleges can be found in most larger communities (or not too far away). Like private driving schools (see the next section), a CDL certificate from a community college shows that you have been well trained, and you have the freedom to choose the job you want.

It takes some time and effort to master the controls of a big rig. *vitpho/iStock/Getty Images*

Private Driving School

Private companies that train truck and bus drivers focus only on that field. They offer training, refresher courses, retraining for a different class of license, and test preparation. You'll have to pay for your program up front, but you'll have the freedom to choose the job you want once you finish the training program. Some private schools work hand in hand with community college programs or employer training programs, which helps provide access, job placement, and tuition remissions.

Company-Sponsored Training

Some companies train drivers themselves, under the watchful eye of an experienced mentor. In addition to learning to drive a commercial vehicle, you also learn that company's way of doing things, their rules and regulations, and their expectations and company culture. Companies may offer "in-house" CDL training or "tuition-sponsored" training through a community college or private driving school.

The big advantage to company-sponsored training is that you already have a job. However, there are some issues to consider before you commit:

- You'll be expected to sign at least a one-year contract. If you leave the company before your contract is over, you may have to pay back the cost of your training when you go.
- It's not always as free as it sounds. You won't have any up-front training costs, *but* the company may expect to recoup the cost of training you by paying you less or deducting the cost from your paycheck over time.
- With company-sponsored training, you might not be training near home. You'll have to pay for living accommodations during your training period.
- Finally, you only learn to use the equipment they use—this may limit your options later on if you want to change jobs.

The College Option

There are many careers associated with ground transportation and the supply chain where a college degree can be helpful or even essential. Some only require a two-year associate degree; others need a four-year bachelor's degree. Moving up into management is easier if you have a master's degree, such as a master of business administration (MBA). Let's consider all the options.

WHAT DEGREE DO YOU NEED?

The kind of degree you pursue and the kind of college or university you attend depends in part on the kind of job you want. If you plan to begin working in the supply chain field at the entry level, you can start with an associate degree. If you'd like to enter the working world at a higher level or in a specialized field, start with a bachelor's degree.

Remember, if you earn an associate degree and later want a bachelor's, you don't have to start from scratch. You've already got two years of college, so you'll only need to finish the remaining credits for your bachelor's degree.

Classroom learning is an important part of education and training for any ground transportation career. *gorodenkoff/iStock/Getty Images*

Associate Degree

Let's begin by looking at associate degree programs for different types of ground transportation careers. Associate degrees are offered through community or technical colleges. Online programs exist for these degrees, but they can't offer the hands-on training that real-life courses do.

You might want an associate degree if you plan to start your ground transportation career in an entry-level supply chain position such as a clerk in manufacturing, retailing, carrier/transportation services, warehouse operations, or purchasing/transportation management. Associate degrees usually take two years (or in college jargon, sixty credit hours).

Associate degrees in ground transportation topics are usually associate of science (AS) or associate of applied science (AAS) degrees with majors such as supply chain management or logistics. They are offered by community colleges and public or private technical schools. Some are designed to let graduates easily transfer to a bachelor's degree.

In most of these programs, you can expect to take general education courses in English, social science, and mathematics. Courses for the major might well include the following:

Community colleges offer a cost-effective, close-to-home learning experience. *crisserbug/iStock/ Getty Images*

- Logistics and international transportation
- Customer service and sales
- Inventory and warehouse management
- Macroeconomics
- Software applications for business
- Principles of purchasing[8]

Bachelor's Degree

According to the Association for Supply Chain Management (ASCM), about 54 percent of people in the field between ages twenty to twenty-nine who held bachelor's degrees had majored in supply chain management. Another 21 percent took classes in supply chain management while pursuing a different major.[9]

Other majors associated with careers in ground transportation and the supply chain include the following:

Bachelor's and master's degrees will take you farther along on the ground transportation career road. *JohnnyH5/iStock/Getty Images*

- Business
- Logistics
- Operations management
- Management sciences and information systems
- Transportation engineering
- Transportation management
- Industrial engineering

Master's Degree

The most commonly held master's degree for people in supply chain professions is the master of business administration (MBA).[10] Other possible master's degrees include a master of arts (MA) in transportation and logistics management, or advanced degrees in engineering.

CHOOSING THE RIGHT COLLEGE PROGRAM FOR YOU

There are all kinds of things to compare and consider when you're choosing a college program.

Admissions Requirements

Admissions requirements are those things you need to have in place in order to apply to and enroll in the college of your choice. When you're considering a two-year or four-year college program, be sure you go to the Admissions page of their website and find out what the requirements are. The following is a list of what's most likely, but again, each individual college is a little bit different, so don't skip the websites.

Community College: Certificate or Associate Degree Program

- High school diploma or GED
- Free Application for Federal Student Aid (FAFSA); see the "Financial Aid" section later in this chapter
- No SAT or ACT exams ("open admissions")
- Possibly a placement test to help you choose appropriate coursework
- Residency requirements may apply

Technical College: Certificate or Associate Degree Program

- Possible age requirements (sixteen, seventeen, or eighteen)
- High school diploma or GED
- Placement test
- Entrance exam (different programs may or may not require one)
- Acceptable entrance exam scores often means you can skip the placement exam
- Residency requirement may apply

Four-Year College or University: Bachelor's Degree

Most four-year colleges and universities do not have open admissions, so the application requirements are more extensive. Be aware of application deadlines. While community colleges admit everyone, four-year colleges may turn down applicants if they don't have room in a particular program or if the applicant doesn't show enough academic promise.

For students applying to a four-year college or university program straight out of high school, you will most likely be expected to provide the following:

- High school diploma or GED, or high school transcripts if you haven't graduated yet
- Usually an SAT or ACT exam (a few four-year colleges have stopped asking for these)
- Sometimes one or more SAT subject tests
- Essay(s) and sometimes short answers to prompts
- Recommendations (two or three letters)
- Application fee
- Common App form or something similar
- Proof of residency (for state colleges and universities)
- Résumé

Transfer students are those who already have an associate degree from a community or technical college, or those who have completed college-level coursework at another school and want to have those credits counted toward their bachelor's degree. Some of these requirements may be waived for applicants with associate degrees or enough transfer credits.

ACADEMIC ENVIRONMENT

Does the school offer the majors or certificate programs you want? Does it have the right level of degree program? What percent of classes are taught by professors, and what percent are taught by adjunct instructors? Are adjunct instructors working professionals in the field? Does the school offer internships, cooperative education programs, or help to find jobs? Does the coursework match up with state standards and codes?

FINANCIAL AID OPTIONS

This is something you have to look at carefully—see the "Financial Aid" section below. Some employers will pay the cost of coursework taken by their employees. If you get a deal like that, you won't need to worry about financial aid. But not every employer can or will make that offer. Some expect reimbursement for the courses they pay for. And some don't provide an educational benefit at all.

Don't worry if you need financial aid. Scholarships and grants may be available as well as loans. Does your college provide access to scholarships, grants, work-study jobs, or other opportunities? How much does the cost of school play a role in your decision?

SUPPORT SERVICES

Support services include things like academic counseling, career counseling, health and wellness, residence services, the financial aid office, information technology support, commuter services, and services for students who are disabled, or who have families, or who are lesbian, gay, bisexual, or transgender. Some schools also have religious services, such as a chaplain. Before you choose a school, look through the website and be sure it provides the services you will need.

CLUBS/ACTIVITIES/SOCIAL LIFE

Most colleges have clubs and other social activities on campus, whether the student population is composed of mostly residents or mostly commuters. Look for clubs related to the major you're interested in, as well as clubs and activities that meet your other interests. College campuses have all kinds of things going on all the time, for students and for the local community—concerts, comics, plays, open mic nights, game nights, art shows, and lots of other things. Don't miss out!

SPECIALIZED PROGRAMS

Does the school or program you're looking at have any programs that meet your specialized needs? For instance, some institutions have programs specifically for veterans. Some address learning disabilities or mental health issues. If you might benefit from a specialized program like these, be sure the school you attend can meet that need.

HOUSING OPTIONS

What kind of housing options do you want and need? Does the college provide dorms? How many students will share a room? Are there on-campus apartments? Is there help with finding off-campus housing like apartments or rooms for rent? Some community and technical colleges mostly serve students who live off campus and commute for classes. Be sure you have an affordable place to live.

TRANSPORTATION

If you live off campus, how will you get to school? Is there a bus system—campus or municipal? Is there a ride-share program? Could you ride a bicycle? Will you need to have access to a car? Is there an on-campus shuttle bus service that can get you around quickly if you're attending a large campus? Is there enough student parking?

STUDENT BODY

What's the makeup of the student body? Is there enough diversity? Are most of the students residents or commuters? Part time or full time? Who will you meet? College is a great place to meet and get to know other people who share your interests. It's also a great place to meet and get to know people who are very different from you. On a college campus, you'll encounter people from small towns and large cities who are of different ethnic backgrounds, different genders, and different ages and who are studying or teaching many different topics. Be sure you take advantage of the opportunity to discover more kinds of people.

THE RIGHT FIT

One of the most important characteristics of a college program is finding the right "fit." What does that mean? It means finding the school that not only offers the program you want but also feels right. Many students have no idea what they're looking for in a school until they walk onto the campus for a visit. Suddenly, they'll say to themselves, "This is the one!"

While you're evaluating a particular institution's offerings with your conscious mind, your unconscious mind is also at work, gathering information about all kinds of things at lightning speed. When it tells your conscious mind what it's decided, we call that a "gut reaction." Pay attention to your gut reactions. There's good information in there.

WHAT'S IT GOING TO COST YOU?

Costs can be quite different, depending on the field you want to go into and the program you choose.

Annual Costs—Undergraduate College/University

Table 3.1 is from the College Board's *Trends in College Pricing and Student Aid 2020*[11] and compares expenses at different kinds of colleges.

Table 3.1.   Expenses at Various Colleges

| | Sector | | | | | Carnegie Classification | | | | | |
| | | | | | | Public Four-Year | | | Private Nonprofit Four-Year | | |
	Public Two-Year In-District	Public Four-Year In-State	Public Four-Year Out-of-State	Private Nonprofit Four-Year	For-Profit	Doctoral	Master's	Bachelor's	Doctoral	Master's	Bachelor's
Tuition and Fees											
2020-21	$3,770	$10,560	$27,020	$37,650	—	$11,440	$8,950	$8,760	$44,910	$29,670	$37,500
2019-20	$3,700	$10,440	$26,770	$36,880	$15,400	$11,290	$8,860	$8,690	$43,630	$29,520	$36,700
$ Change	$70	$120	$250	$770	—	$150	$90	$70	$1,280	$150	$800
% Change	1.9%	1.1%	0.9%	2.1%	—	1.3%	1.0%	0.8%	2.9%	0.5%	2.2%
Room and Board (RB)											
2020-21 (estimated)	$9,080	$11,620	$11,620	$13,120		$12,110	$10,680	$10,840	$14,930	$12,360	$12,140
2019-20	$8,990	$11,510	$11,510	$12,990	—	$11,990	$10,580	$10,730	$14,780	$12,240	$12,020
Tuition and Fees and Room and Board											
2020-21 (with estimated RB)	$12,850	$22,180	$38,640	$50,770	—	$23,550	$19,630	$19,600	$59,840	$42,030	$49,640
2019-20	$12,690	$21,950	$38,280	$49,870	—	$23,280	$19,440	$19,420	$58,410	$41,760	$48,720
Percentage of Undergraduates Enrolled Full Time											
Fall 2018	35%	81%		83%	67%	84%	76%	57%	87%	75%	88%

NOTES: Prices in Table 1 are not adjusted for inflation. Tuition prices reported for 2019-20 have been revised and may differ from those reported in Trends in College Pricing 2019. Average room and board prices for 2020-21 are not available because of the evolving campus opening status across institutions in the United States in fall 2020. The latest tuition and fee estimate available for the for-profit sector is for 2019-20.

SOURCES: College Board, Annual Survey of Colleges; NCES, IPEDS Fall 2018 Enrollment data and IPEDS 2019 Institutional Characteristics data.

Enrollment-weighted tuition and fees weight the price charged by each institution by the number of full-time undergraduate students enrolled in fall 2018. Public four-year in-state charges are weighted by total fall 2018 full-time undergraduate enrollment in each institution, including both in-state students and out-of-state students. Out-of-state tuition and fees are computed by adding the average in-state price to the out-of-state premium weighted by the number of full-time out-of-state undergraduate students enrolled at each institution. Room and board charges are weighted by the number of undergraduate students residing on campus for four-year institutions and by the number of commuter students for public two-year institutions.

This table was prepared in October 2020.

The following chart is From the College Board's Trends in College Pricing and Student Aid 2020, comparing expenses at different kinds of colleges.

That's a lot of money! *However*, these are averages. And note the difference in cost between a year at a two-year community or technical college and a year at a four-year college or university. In general, tuition and other costs for college tend to go up about 3 percent every year, so take that into consideration when planning for the year that you'll be going to school. You'll need to look closely at the costs of the schools you're considering—they could be quite different from these.

There are all kinds of ways to get those costs down.

Financial Aid

It is worth your while to put some time and effort into finding out what financial aid you qualify for. Reach out to the financial aid office at the school you want to attend. They can tell you a lot about what you may be able to work out.

Financial aid can come from many sources. The kind of awards you're eligible for depend on a lot of things, such as the following:

- Academic performance in high school
- Financial need
- Program/field
- Type of college

Follow up on financial aid for affordable higher education. *designer491/iStock/Getty Images*

NOT ALL FINANCIAL AID IS CREATED EQUAL

Educational institutions tend to define financial aid as any scholarship, grant, loan, or paid employment that assists students to pay their college expenses. Notice that "financial aid" covers both *money you have to pay back* and *money you don't have to pay back*. That's a big difference!

FUNDS THAT DO NOT HAVE TO BE REPAID

- Scholarships
- Grants
- Work-study

FUNDS THAT HAVE TO BE REPAID *WITH INTEREST*

- Federal government loans
- Private loans
- Institutional loans

Tuition Benefits

Before you apply for scholarships or loans, first find out if you are eligible for money for classes from outside sources.

Employer Tuition Benefit

Some employers are willing to pay some or all of the cost of coursework for their employees. This isn't something every employer can afford, but if you are trying to choose among several employment options, a course tuition benefit can be an important factor in helping you decide. Even if they can only contribute a small amount, every bit helps. Be sure you understand if there are any "strings attached" to your employer's tuition benefit. Some require that you stay with the company for a certain period of time (that's not unreasonable). Some expect you to pay back the tuition benefit over time through payroll deduction or lower wages.

Union Tuition Benefit

Are you in a union? As with employers, benefits vary from union to union and state to state. But unions provide important benefits to their members, and education is often one of them.

Scholarships

Scholarships are financial awards that are usually offered on the basis of academic merit, membership in a particular organization, or for going into a specific field. Scholarships can also be available to students who have certain characteristics, such as athletes, or who are part of a group that is underrepresented in a particular field or major. Some scholarships go toward tuition; others are for something specific, like textbooks and school supplies.

Scholarships usually pay a portion of tuition—it is very rare to receive a full-tuition scholarship, but it does happen. Scholarships do not have to be paid back. Scholarships can be local, regional, statewide, or national in scope.

Be sure to check with your high school guidance counselor as well as the school you're planning to attend. Some high schools have scholarships that go to graduating seniors who are planning to pursue a particular job. There are also scholarships specifically for community or technical college students, including those who want to transfer to a bachelor's degree program later on or those who are studying a particular subject. Some are offered by professional associations, some by nonprofit organizations, and some by the community colleges themselves.

To learn more about scholarships, check out www.gocollege.com/financial -aid/scholarships/types/.

Grants

Grants are similar to scholarships. Most tuition grants are awarded based on financial need, but some are restricted to students in particular sports, academic fields, or demographic groups, or with special talents. Grants do not have to be paid back.

Some grants come through federal or state agencies, such as the Pell Grant, SMART Grants, and Federal Supplemental Education Opportunity Grant (FSEOG). You'll need to fill out the FAFSA form (see the section "Loans" below). Learn more about those at studentaid.ed.gov/types/grants-scholarships.

Grants can also come from private organizations or from the college itself. For instance, some private colleges or universities have enough financial resources that they can "meet 100 percent of proven financial need." That doesn't mean a free ride, but it usually means some grant money to cover the gap between what the financial aid office believes you can afford and the amount covered by scholarships and federal loans (more on federal loans below).

Work-Study

The federal work-study program provides money for undergraduate and graduate students to earn money through part-time jobs. Work-study is a need-based program, so you'll need to find out if you are eligible for it. Some students are not eligible at first but become eligible later in their college career. Most jobs are on campus; some relate to your field, but others—like working in the library—could be more general.

Some colleges and universities don't participate in the work-study program, so check with the financial aid office to see if it's available and if you're eligible for it. It's good to apply early to have a better chance of getting the job you want most.

Since work-study is earned money (you do a job and get paid for it), this money does not need to be paid back. To learn more, check out studentaid .ed.gov/sa/types/work-study.

Loans

There is almost always a gap between tuition and the amount of money you receive from a school in scholarships and grants. That gap is filled by student loans. Student loans have to be repaid. Interest varies depending on the type of loan. Be sure you understand how much interest you will be charged, when the interest starts to accumulate, and when you must start paying the loan back. Usually, repayment starts when you graduate or after a six-month grace period.

Federal Loans

Federal student loans are issued by the U.S. government. They have lower interest rates and better repayment terms than other loans. You don't need anyone to cosign for your debt. If the loan is subsidized, the federal government pays the interest until you graduate. If it's unsubsidized, interest starts to accrue as soon as you accept the loan. That can amount to a very big difference in how much you pay for your education by the time the loan is paid off.

The most common federal student loan is the low-interest Federal Stafford Loan, which is available to both undergraduate and graduate students. Depending on household income, a student's Stafford loan might be subsidized or unsubsidized.

Most schools will require you to fill out the FAFSA when you apply for financial aid. FAFSA stands for Free Application for Federal Student Aid. Note that it doesn't say "free student aid." It says "free application." That means it does not cost anything to apply for federal student aid. You may get "offers" to submit the FAFSA for you for a fee—this is a scam. Don't do it.

Private Loans

Private student loans are issued by a bank or other financial institution. Rates of interest are generally higher than for federal loans, so be careful not to borrow more than you need. Eligibility criteria for private loans are based on your credit (and your cosigner's credit) history. Don't just take the first loan you find. Do some research and compare interest rates and terms. Is the interest variable or fixed? Is there a cap on the variable interest? Is the company reputable? What are their repayment requirements?

Institutional Loans

Many educational institutions make their own loans, using funds provided by donors such as alumni, corporations, and foundations, as well as from repayments made by prior college loan borrowers. Every college will have its own rules, terms, eligibility, and rates. Interest may be lower than private student loans, and deferment option may be better as well.

Learn more about all kinds of financial aid through the College Board website at bigfuture.collegeboard.org/pay-for-college.

FINANCIAL AID TIPS

- Some colleges/universities will offer tuition discounts or grants to encourage students to attend—so tuition costs can be lower than they look at first.
- Apply for financial aid during your senior year of high school. The sooner you apply, the better your chances. Check out fafsa.gov to see how to get started.
- Compare offers from different schools—one school may be able to match or improve on another school's financial aid offer.
- Keep your grades up—a good GPA helps a lot when it comes to merit scholarships and grants.
- You have to reapply for financial aid every year, so you'll be filling out that FAFSA form again.
- Look for ways that loans might be deferred or forgiven—service commitment programs are a way to use service to pay back loans.

Summary

Whether you take the training route to prepare for a ground transportation job that doesn't require a college degree, or you head to a two-year or four-year college program to get the education you need for a supply chain or logistics job, there are so many options for you. Be sure to take the time to understand your choices, so you can choose the path that will work best for you and your goals.

Next, let's take a look at what happens after you complete your education and training. What goes into getting a job in ground transportation? And what do you need to know to be successful in your chosen career?

Follow the education path on to your real goal: a career in ground transportation! *Porcorex/iStock/ Getty Images*

ED MANKOSKI, COMMERCIAL VEHICLE INSTRUCTOR

Ed Mankoski. *Courtesy of Ed Mankoski*

Ed Mankoski has been driving straight trucks and tractor-trailers for more than forty years. After a long career with one trucking company, Ed now brings all that experience to his students as an instructor for the Commercial Vehicle Transportation (CVT) program at Hagerstown Community College in Maryland. He continues to drive a tractor-trailer for FedEx Ground as well.

How did you become an instructor with the CVT program at Hagerstown Community College?
I got interested in trucking when I was six or seven years old. My dad was a steel hauler in Chicago in the sixties and he'd sneak me

along. After high school, I started driving, too. In 2011, I'd been with a local trucking company for twenty-six years. I decided to leave there for a change of scenery, so I went to a job fair at Hagerstown Community College to see what else I could do. I saw they had the CVT program, and I said, "You wouldn't happen to be looking for a truck driving instructor, would you?" Turns out they were. They said, "Yes," and that's how I got here.

What is a typical day on your job?
We'll start the first day with in-cab and outside pre-trips. Then we move on to the skills. By the second or third week, we're starting to actually drive. Then it becomes a repetition. The last three weeks is practicing what we learned in the first three weeks. It's a seven-and-a-half-week course that runs Monday to Friday, which is what I'm doing. We also have a weekend course that's fifteen weeks. It's a three-hundred-hour course, either way, which includes classroom and behind-the-wheel time. Behind the wheel, they're getting four to five hundred miles of driving time.

What's the best part of working with the CVT program?
Two of my former students happened to drop in today! That's the most rewarding part—when I see my former students here or on Facebook. When I see how they're doing, it's the most rewarding part of my job. Seeing the people I help to get to where they're at.

What's the most challenging part of working with the CVT program?
We get a lot of students that have never driven a manual transmission going to driving a tractor-trailer that weighs 30,000 pounds empty. Having to get them acclimated to doing that from driving a car with an automatic transmission, or even a car with a manual transmission—it's not like driving a truck. Pre-trip is just memorization; skills are just going backward and forward. But the driving part with shifting and making turns, it's a lot tougher and more stressful than anyone thinks of before they start doing it.

What's the most surprising thing about working with the CVT program?
I knew a little bit about the program because the company I worked for usually got students from Hagerstown Community College. They weren't all A-list truckers, but we got better students from here than from other schools. It was a good program before, and now it's even better. Everyone works together as a team: the coordinator, the assistant coordinator, the other instructors, all the students. I'm surprised it works as flawlessly as it does.

How did your education and experience prepare you for your role in the CVT program?

I graduated high school, but I didn't have any college background until I was working in the office of the trucking company. Then I took some management courses. The fact that I have been a driver and I'm currently a driver has been really helpful. When I first started, there were four other guys teaching who were really helpful to me in learning how to teach it. I knew how to do it, but I hadn't had a lot of exposure to how you teach it. You put your own spin on it. I show the new instructors what I do, we start and end at the same place in the syllabus, but we all have our own spin on how we do it. And the students. Everyone learns differently, so you have to teach differently depending on what the need is.

Is working with the CVT program what you expected?

Yes, pretty much. As I said, I had a little exposure to it from the students we got at the trucking company. I'd say I'd rate it an eight or nine out of ten in terms of what I thought it was going to be.

What's next? Where do you see yourself going from here?

Retirement! I turn sixty-three soon and I'm looking to scale my workload down. For a while I was working four part-time jobs: working here, for FedEx, in a recycling center, and at a ski resort in the winter. So I'm planning to get that down to one job by the time I'm sixty-five.

Where do you see careers in ground transportation going in the future?

I hear my students talking about self-driving trucks and trains, but I don't think it's going to happen in my lifetime or my students' lifetimes. We're going to need trucks to move things around. We haven't done that good of a job with self-driving cars, so I don't think we're going to have self-driving trucks soon. We have new technology now, though, that I wouldn't have thought would have existed when I started driving in the eighties.

What is your advice for a young person considering this career path?

First, there are always jobs. We have fourteen recruiters that come to our school every term. There are two-dozen trucking companies that hire right out of our school. I've trained people from age seventeen to seventy, people who were store managers or had their own businesses. There are people from all walks of life—age, race, gender, you name it—who've come through here. It's like a lot of jobs—if you put the effort into it, you can make a lot of money for it. But it's not a forty-hour week. If you're lucky, it's sixty or even seventy hours, six or seven days a week. If you're good at it, you can make a lot of money and there's always jobs. But you have to find out what's the best fit for you. I tell my students, what's your motivator? Is it money, home time, benefits? Talk to your spouse or your partner and figure out what works best for you. Then try to match that up with a company. There are so many companies. My students come and ask me about this company or that company, and I could tell them what I think, but what's right for one isn't right for another. When I started driving in my twenties, money and newer equipment were the most important things. When I was older, retirement benefits became more important.

======

Writing Your Résumé and Interviewing

Putting It All Together and Getting the Job

You've done your planning and chosen a career in ground transportation. You've done your research and determined what you want to do and where you want to go. You've prepared yourself with your education and training, and you've developed your practical skills as well as your knowledge of the job. And you know that working in ground transportation is a great career with lots of opportunity.

Which job will be right for you? *IPGGutenbergUKLtd/iStock/Getty Images*

So how do you turn all that preparation into an actual job? In this chapter, we're going to take a look at the other skills you need to get not just *a* job, but *the* job. Those are the business skills that everyone needs to have to be successful.

Where to Find the Jobs

EMPLOYERS HAVE TO FOLLOW RULES, TOO

Kameleon007/iStock/Getty Images

Once you have your commercial driver's license (CDL), you'll be looking for a company that hires CDL drivers. At the very least, any company that hires CDL drivers must meet the following standards from the Federal Motor Carrier Safety Administration (FMCSA). There are different rules for companies engaged in intrastate commerce (i.e., all driving is within one state) versus interstate commerce (driving across state lines).

- **USDOT number:** This is a unique number from the U.S. Department of Transportation that the FMCSA uses when it's reviewing compliance or conducting inspections or investigations.
- **Operating authority:** This shows what kind of cargo or passengers you carry, and what geographical areas the company can legally operate in.

- **Notifications:** Companies must ask for job applicants' employment history for the last ten years. Companies may not knowingly employ a driver who has multiple licenses; whose license has been suspended, canceled, or revoked; or who is disqualified from driving.
- **Certification:** Some states allow companies to administer CDL tests if they are certified to do so. They must meet FMCSA minimum guidelines and use the same tests that their state uses. The state and FMCSA both have the right to do random inspections, audits, and examinations.
- **Penalties:** According to the North American Uniform Out-of-Service Criteria, a driver, a commercial motor vehicle, or motor carrier operation is declared "out of service" based on criteria relating to "imminent hazard" in the transport of materials. The company has to pay stiff fines for out-of-service violations as determined by an authorized enforcement officer of a federal, state, Canadian, Mexican, or local jurisdiction.
- In addition, each state may have their own procedures, rules, fees, and renewal/reinstatement procedures for companies who employ CDL drivers.[1]

Résumés and Applications

Everyone needs a résumé. Even if the job you're applying for requires you to fill in an application form (online or on paper), all the information you need will be at your fingertips on your résumé. You never know when a new opportunity will come up. Be ready to respond by keeping your résumé up to date.

WHAT IS A RÉSUMÉ?

A résumé is a simple way to list everything you've done that has prepared you for the job you're applying for. It includes sections for your education, your training, and your previous experience. It may also include any honors you've earned or special things you've done or been a part of.

You submit your résumé (along with a cover letter) whenever you apply for a job. You may also want to upload your résumé to a few of the many résumé sites available on the internet. A résumé should be one to two pages long.

Keep your résumé up to date so you're ready for any opportunity. *Mihailomilovanovic/E+/Getty Images*

TYPES OF RÉSUMÉS

There are three basic formats for a résumé:

- Reverse chronological résumé
- Functional résumé
- Combined résumé

You may want to use a different type of résumé for different times or stages in your career. Once you've got a lot of experience or want to move up to management, for instance, you'll want to highlight the specific skills you've acquired that qualify you for that role.

Reverse Chronological Résumé

This is the most traditional format for a résumé. A reverse chronological résumé is written with the most current information first, going backwards to the oldest information last. This type of résumé works for everyone, whether you're a student, an entry-level applicant, or an experienced ground transportation worker. It's simple to copy the information from a reverse chronological résumé into an application form.

The usual layout for a reverse chronological résumé is pretty simple.

- Name and contact information at the top.
- Education, starting with most recent first.
- If you went to college, you don't need to list high school.
- When you're at the beginning of your career, list education first; when you're more experienced, move the education section after the experience section.
- Qualifications such as certification and/or license (e.g., CDL class and all endorsements).
- Professional experience with job title, dates of employment (month or year is fine), and a short, bulleted list of your duties and accomplishments.
- Military service (if any).
- Awards and honors (if any).
- Volunteer experience (if relevant).

Use a reverse chronological résumé under the following circumstances:

- Most of your experience has been in one field.
- Your work history demonstrates a clear career path.
- You work in a field that doesn't accept functional résumés.
- You want to include your résumé in an online jobs database or job search website.
- You expect to fill in application forms.

Functional Résumé

A functional résumé is designed to highlight your skills and qualifications rather than your work history. Also called a skills résumé, the functional résumé shows that you're a strong candidate for a job and plays down periods of time when you weren't employed or were working in an unrelated field. A functional résumé helps employers focus on specific skills needed for the job they're hiring for. It's all about making sure the employer can focus on what's relevant to the job in question.

For a functional résumé, break up your information into several categories that describe your skills. The categories should be in the order of most importance to the *potential employer*. Within each category, include a bulleted list of examples. These should also be in order of importance, rather than by date. Include a synopsis of your work experience. The usual layout for a functional résumé is as follows:

- Name and contact information at the top.
- Summary of your skills and abilities.
- Qualifications such as certification and license.
- Relevant skill blocks in order of importance—such as technical skills, business skills, and people skills—with short examples.
- Professional experience with job title and dates of employment (month or year is fine). Include short, bulleted items about your duties and accomplishments if the jobs are different from each other in a significant way (otherwise you've already covered this in the skill blocks).
- Awards and honors (if any).
- Education, starting with most recent first (if you've been to college, you don't need to list high school).
- Volunteer experience (if relevant).

Use a functional résumé under the following circumstances:

- You want to tailor your résumé to a particular job opening.
- You have less experience.
- You have highly specialized experience.
- You have gaps in your employment history.
- You have changed jobs frequently or after a short period of time.

Combined Résumé

A combined résumé is the best of both worlds. It puts together aspects of both the reverse chronological résumé and the functional résumé. A combined résumé is best for someone who has developed some experience, so that you have something to summarize. It summarizes your skills while still showing your impressive employment history.

Like a functional résumé, the combined résumé begins with a professional summary of your skills, abilities, and achievements that are specifically relevant to the job opening. Then your education and experience follow in reverse chronological order.

The usual layout for a combined résumé is pretty simple:

- Name and contact information at the top.
- Summary of your skills and abilities.
- Qualifications such as certification and licensing.
- Professional experience with job title and dates of employment (month or year is fine). Include short, bulleted items about your duties and accomplishments if the jobs are different from each other in a significant way (otherwise you've already covered this in the skill blocks).
- Awards and honors (if any).
- Education and/or training.
- Volunteer experience (if relevant).

Use a combined résumé under the following circumstances:

- You have a lot of experience and want to focus on your knowledge and accomplishments.
- You want to highlight your relevant experience.
- You're applying for a job that requires technical skills and expertise.
- You want to move into a new field.
- You want to demonstrate mastery in your field.

Writing Your Cover Letter

Your cover letter is an opportunity to tell your story. It's a short, personalized letter that you send with your résumé to introduce yourself to a potential employer. A well-written cover letter is a way to show a little of your personality, to highlight where and how your background makes a good fit for the position you want, and to indicate your interest in working for that employer.

You should always try to send your letter and résumé together to the person who is responsible for making the hiring decision. If (and *only* if) you absolutely cannot find out who the decision maker is, then send them to the human resources office.

Your letter should be in business letter format with the following items:

- Your name and contact information (mailing address, phone number, and e-mail address) go at the top of the letter, either centered or on the right.
- Address the reader by name—avoid generic greetings like "Dear Manager" or "Dear Director." Use *Ms.* or *Mr.* with the last name. (Do not use *Miss* or *Mrs.* unless you have been specifically instructed to do so.) Only use the first name if you have met the person and they specifically told you to call them by their first name.
- Identify the specific position you are interested in, and where you heard about it (some companies like to track how applicants heard about the position). Mention that your résumé is included or attached.
- If you heard about the opening from a specific person, mention them by name.
- Highlight your most relevant qualifications: skills that match the ones in the job description and/or skills that could transfer to those in the job description. Focus on your strengths and on what you could bring to the position. Think about this *from the employer's point of view*—what about your background will benefit them?
- Avoid negative language—phrase everything in a positive way. In particular, avoid complaining about a previous employer or customer.
- Your conclusion should include a confident call to action, such as requesting an interview. Don't ask directly for the job, just an interview at this point. Include your phone number here, as well as with your contact information at the top.
- Closing: *Sincerely,* (That's it. Don't use any other word.)
- Add a few lines of space for your signature, then type your name.
- Sign the letter by hand.

Application Forms

Many companies offer an application form—either their own or a generic form provided by an online résumé or hiring service. As long as you keep your résumé up to date, you'll have all the information you need to quickly fill in these forms.

There are also online forms for résumé sites where you can upload your résumé for employers to see. If you attend a two- or four-year college program, the Alumni Office may maintain a résumé bank like this.

Online application forms make it easy to apply for jobs. *Hiraman/E+/Getty Images*

ONLINE APPLICATION FORMS

Online application forms make things easier for applicants and employers. One advantage is that you can often copy and paste information out of your résumé from your computer directly into the right box on the form.

Online forms can be a little "unforgiving" about what information they want and how they want you to provide it.

- Be sure to fill in all the boxes that are required—these are often marked with an asterisk (*).
- Fill in nonrequired boxes as best you can.

- If there is a place to upload your résumé, do that as well as filling in the form. If you can save your résumé as a PDF document, your formatting will be protected (the reader will see the document the same way that you do).
- Online forms are not perfect. For instance, if they ask for a letter, a résumé, and a list of references but only give you a place to upload the résumé, try saving all the documents together (in that order) in a PDF file. You can then upload them as one file.
- Be sure you have filled in *everything* correctly before you hit SEND. Sometimes application forms will have a SAVE option so that you can come back to the form and make changes before you finally hit SEND.
- If you have any trouble with the form, call the company (usually the human resources or personnel office) and ask for help.

PAPER APPLICATION FORMS

Paper application forms are a lot less common than they once were, but you still encounter them, especially at smaller employers. You'll need to copy information by hand from your résumé onto the paper form.

- Write neatly! Paper forms are read by people. Keep it in the boxes.
- Fill in all required information.
- Fill in as much nonrequired information as you have.
- See if you can attach your cover letter and your résumé.
- Paper application forms are usually filled in on site, at the potential employer's office, so if you have a problem or a question about the form, there may be someone you can ask. Be sure to ask!
- Be sure everything on the form is correct before you turn it in.
- If you make a mess of the form, with lots of changes and crossing out, ask for a new form and fill it in neatly.

GETTING TO YES

There is a lot of work at all levels in the ground transportation sector of the supply chain, and you will most likely find a job. But there's no guarantee that you will be offered the job you want most when you first start looking. The following is a list of some tips that will improve your chances of "getting to yes":

- Do your research—find out about the company that you want to apply to.
- Talk to people—especially people you know already or friends of friends who know something about that employer.
- Ask about what the potential employer is like to work for.
- Ask about what they value in their employees.
- Ask about benefits and the general pros and cons of working there.
- If there is a specific job opening you're qualified for, apply for it.
- If there isn't a specific job opening, send a letter to the head of the company or department you're interested in, mention your contacts, and ask if they would have a conversation with you about potential openings.
- Be flexible—you might find a good job in a different location than you wanted, or doing something slightly different than you originally planned.
- Put your best self forward—everyone you meet is a potential contact for a job (or maybe just a new friend).
- If you get an interview, don't forget that all-important thank-you note. It's one of the most important things you can do to make a good impression. Send the note that day, as soon after the interview as possible.
- Don't put all your eggs in one basket—apply for numerous jobs at the same time.

DEALING WITH NO

A wise person once said, "If they didn't hire you, you probably would not have been happy working there anyway." Both employers and employees need to find the right fit. If they didn't think you were the right fit, you most likely wouldn't have thought so after a while, either. The following is a list of some tips to get you through a "No" while you're waiting for the "Yes."

- Apply for lots of jobs at the same time, so no particular job will be too important to you.
- It doesn't feel great to be turned down for a job, but try not to take it personally.
- Don't burn your bridges! Don't retaliate with an angry letter or e-mail, or troll the company all over social media. Another opportunity may come up there or with someone they know.
- Keep improving your résumé and your cover letter.
- Keep putting your best self forward—even if you're feeling discouraged, pick yourself up and go through your day shining with confidence.
- Work your contacts—talk to other people you know. They may know an employer who would be a great match for you.
- Take advice—if someone (especially at or following an interview) tells you that you need to improve something, *improve it*. This may be an additional credential, it may be something about your interpersonal skills or your spelling or your breath or whatever. If someone tells you something about yourself that you don't like to hear but suspect may be right, don't get mad. Get better.
- Keep doing your research, so if one employer turns you down, you have three more to apply to that day.
- Keep telling yourself that employment is just around the corner. Then make it true!

No matter what field you go into, people skills are important. We never know, really, when we're younger where life is going to take us.—Brian Bragdon

The Interview

An interview is a business meeting where a prospective employer is checking you out. Don't forget that you are also checking them out. You are both there to see if it would be a good fit for you to work together. No matter how much you want the job, remember that you are not there to beg for charity—you are there to offer your services in your professional role.

Be your best self at your interview. *SDI Productions/iStock/Getty Images*

INTERVIEWING TIPS

- **Be on time:** Don't be late, *ever*. Try to arrive ten to fifteen minutes early so you have time to go into the restroom and check yourself in the mirror before you go into the interview. And don't be too early—that's just awkward.
- **Be polished:** See the section below on how to dress.
- **Bring your résumé:** Yes, they already have it. Bring extra copies just in case. It's helpful and shows that you're the kind of person who is prepared.
- **Smile:** Let them know that you will be a pleasant person to work with.
- **Shake hands well:** Traditionally, a firm handshake marked you as a person to be taken seriously, so you would shake hands as you come into the interview, and again before you leave. After COVID-19, many people are wary of shaking hands. Either way, the person giving the interview decides whether to offer to shake hands, so you don't need to put out your hand first.
- **Ask for a business card:** You may meet with just one person, with a committee, or with several people individually. At the end of the meeting, ask for a business card from each person so that you have good contact information for your thank-you notes.
- **Have good posture:** Sit up straight, make reasonable eye contact (not staring), and keep your shoulders back. Make it look normal, though— like you always sit or stand that way. Good posture conveys energy and enthusiasm for the job, as well as showing you have the physical strength to do the job.
- **Be prepared:** Learn about the company ahead of time so that you sound knowledgeable during the interview. Read their website and talk to people.
- **Be ready to answer questions:** At a job interview, you can expect to get asked some standard questions ("Where do you see yourself in five years?") and questions about the specific job that show you know your stuff.
- **Don't be afraid to ask questions:** Some people don't like to ask questions in an interview because they think it makes them look ignorant. Actually, *not* asking questions makes them look uninterested. Have

some questions prepared—both basic and more in depth, because the basic ones might get answered before you have a chance to ask them.

- **Stay off your phone:** Do we really have to say it? If you're looking at your phone during an interview, you'll look like you don't care. Nobody wants to hire someone who doesn't care before the job even starts!

WHAT TO WEAR

There's an old saying in business: "Don't dress for the job you have. Dress for the job you want." That's never more true than at a job interview.

Office Jobs

So what should you wear for an interview for an office job? The answer is easy—business clothes. A suit is always a good idea. If you don't have a suit, you should consider investing in at least one (if someone wants to buy you a graduation gift, this is an option!). If not, wear dress pants or skirt with a nice blazer-type jacket. Wear a solid-color shirt so your tie or scarf won't clash. Wear business shoes—not sneakers or hiking boots.

You should be neatly groomed. Your hands should be clean, especially your fingernails. Your hair should be freshly washed and arranged in a neat and tidy way. Your clothes should be clean, pressed, and well fitting, without spots, rips, or tears. If you wear any jewelry, keep it to a minimum. If you have tattoos, keep them covered. Be sure your shoes are clean and polished. Avoid perfumes, colognes, or body sprays.

If you have a briefcase, put a few copies of your résumé in it, and bring it along.

Non-Office Jobs

If you're applying for a job out of the office, such as driving a truck or a bus, what should you wear to a job interview? The answer is "business casual," which can mean different things for different places. You don't need to be fancy, but you should be presentable.

- If you're applying for an entry-level job with a smaller company, you could wear khaki pants (aka chinos, but not cargo pants) or good jeans and a nice, button-down shirt or blouse.
- Keep accessories simple.
- Limo driver applicants should dress more formally because appearance is part of the job.
- Wear shoes appropriate to the job, but be sure they're clean and look cared for.
- *Always* be clean and neat for an interview. Brush your teeth. Shower, wash your hair, have a fresh haircut or pull long hair back neatly. Avoid cologne and the smell of cigarettes. Don't chew gum.

Note: T-shirts may be appropriate for your workplace, especially worn under coveralls or a uniform, *but* message tees are never appropriate for work. Leave the ones with words, pictures, jokes, political or religious messages, cartoons, and the like at home. What's funny to you might be offensive to a customer, a coworker, or your boss. And being offensive is unprofessional.

What Potential Employers Look For

There are certain qualities that everybody who works in ground transportation should have. During a job interview, potential employers will be assessing you for these characteristics. Ask yourself these questions, and if you think you need to get better at something, then get better!

COMMUNICATION AND SOCIAL SKILLS

- Will you be able to understand the customer's problems, needs, and values?
- Will you be able to work well with your boss and coworkers?
- Do you have active listening skills?
- Do you speak clearly?
- Do you write clearly?
- Do you show politeness, friendliness, and a good attitude?

GOOD WORK ETHIC

- Do you work hard at assigned tasks?
- Do you look for ways to help employers, coworkers, or customers beyond assigned tasks?
- Do you look for ways to improve your performance?
- Are you on time?
- Do you watch the clock to see how soon you can leave?
- Do you show initiative and work to solve problems?

ADAPTABILITY

- Are you flexible about new situations, new rules and regulations, and new or different environments?
- Are you willing and eager to learn the latest developments, processes, procedures, and code updates?
- Can you get along with all kinds of people?

ENTHUSIASM FOR YOUR FIELD

- Are you proud of the work you do?
- Do you like solving problems?
- Do you like helping people?
- Do you have a desire to continue to build your skills and learn new things?

INDUSTRY HEALTH REQUIREMENTS

For many jobs in the ground transportation sector, especially those that involve driving heavy equipment, you must demonstrate that you meet the FMCSA regulations. CDL holders are expected to be able to pass the Department of Transportation (DOT) physical exam. Your best source of information on medical requirements, drug and alcohol testing, and truck and bus driver wellness programs can be found on the FMCSA's own website at https://www.fmcsa.dot.gov/regulations/medical.

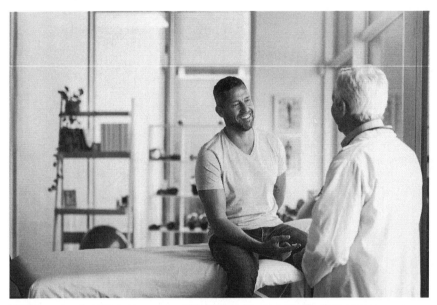

FMCSA requires that CDL holders pass a DOT physical. *Rowan Jordan/E+/Getty Images*

Many employers require that employees be able to pass a drug test and a background check. Think about it—no one wants to find out too late that their employee was impaired while working, endangering themselves and everyone around them. Employers need to be sure that their employees are responsible people—there are a lot of safety issues involved in ground transportation, as well as liability issues. So be sure that you can meet those requirements!

Say Thank You

After any kind of job interview, it is *extremely important* to follow up. This is what shows the other person that you are genuinely interested in the job and in working with them. Write your thank-you note immediately after the interview. Be sure to mention your interest in the job and one or two things from the interview that interested you most. If you met separately with several people, *send each one of them a separate note.*

E-mail is the quickest way to say thank you for an interview. Start with "Dear Ms. Name" (replacing "Name" with whatever their name is) and signing it "Sincerely." Leave two line breaks and then add your name. Since you won't be writing your signature, two line breaks are enough.

On the Job

Now that you've got the job, it's important to keep it. It's not that hard. Just remember these simple tips:

- **Safety first:** Ground transportation jobs deal with hazards all day long. Stay safe and watch out for the safety of those around you. That includes maintaining your health.
- **Do your best:** Your biggest asset is high-quality work.
- **Be reliable:** Your coworkers, customers, and supervisors will respect and appreciate you most when they know they can rely on you.
- **Be on time:** Show up on time for work or even a few minutes early.
- **Be prepared:** Walk in the door ready to work.
- **Keep good records:** This is important for safety as well as efficiency.

Do your best on the job, all the time. *zeljkosantrac/E+/Getty Images*

- **Be polite:** Treat everyone you meet with the same respect you want to receive.
- **Stay calm:** You do your best work when you're calm, especially if there's a problem to solve or an emergency.
- **Have integrity:** Be honest and respect other people's persons and property.

Summary

As long as you do a good job and respect the people you work with and work for, you should have a long and rewarding career. Maybe you'll be driving celebrities or newlyweds in a limousine or taking people to work on a city transit bus. Maybe you'll be transporting goods from one end of the country to another as a long-haul truck driver. Maybe you'll be keeping track of goods coming into and going out of a warehouse, or analyzing and planning the systems that keep those goods moving efficiently around the country. Whatever part of the ground transportation sector you choose, you can be sure you're an important part of the supply chain.

Reliable employees who are good to work with stand out from everyone else. *Comstock/Stockbyte/Getty Images*

Eric Miller, Moving and Storage Company Owner

Eric Miller. *Courtesy of Dragonfly Moving and Storage*

Eric Miller is a managing member of RJ Crowley Moving and Storage and owner/operator of Dragonfly Moving and Storage, both in New Hampshire. After studying at the College of Insurance in Manhattan (now part of St. John's University), Eric spent many years working in the insurance industry; he served as a board member of USA Risk Group, a multinational insurance company that managed 275 insurance companies with clients in seventeen countries and offices in five countries.

How did you become the owner of a moving and storage company?

I was in insurance for thirty years. My life goal was to retire at the age of fifty, which I did—for a little while. Then I started losing my mind! I couldn't do it. I thought, "I've got to go get a job." My wife and I wanted to stay in New Hampshire, and we both wanted me to have a job that didn't require me to travel on airplanes for business. My research showed that the businesses that thrive in New Hampshire are either based on natural resources or provide services that someone must use. In the case of moving and storage, for a large segment of the population this is a necessary service, so as the economic situation varies, our business stays more stable. That's how I gravitated toward this. I looked for a business that wasn't based on a single individual. For a lot of businesses, their individual interaction with the customer is the basis of the business. In this case, the previous owners had passed away and the business was continuing to operate, so that showed the work of the business was necessary. I wanted to honor [previous owner] Bob Crowley's legacy, to come in with the right attitude and approach that the community considered to be honorable, and continue to build on that good reputation. Family dynamics led me to wanting to find a company that was a strong service provider with a strong local reputation.

What is a typical day on your job?

Monday morning at eight in the morning, we have the most perfect schedule ever: we have an equal number of jobs and number of crew. By nine, life has happened.

Closings are delayed, pickups are rescheduled, someone calls in sick. So Monday through Friday, we're trying to dynamically readjust our schedule.

One of the tricks to a successful moving company is to not overwork your guys. You can sprint for a short period of time, but not for the length of a marathon. The way to avoid having people or property break during the day is to make sure you have a reasonable expectation of what your crew can accomplish in a day. That's difficult in an industry where many competitors don't understand that, so you overcome that by having a reputation as the best in the business—the one who pays attention to detail. Asking too much of your crew looks attractive from a financial standpoint, but from a long-term strategy perspective, it's not sustainable. There's an overarching philosophy of making sure that you carefully analyze the jobs coming up and match that to the ability and the equipment and the person-power that you have available to accomplish that job. In the height of our season, we probably decline more business than any other moving company in the state of New Hampshire. Only going for short-term gains means you're creating instability in your employees that will come back to haunt you. For example, my crews only work on the weekend when they're on overtime. That's because for thirty years I worked as much as seventy hours a week. One of the promises I made to my wife is that I would not make her a "work widow" again. I want that for my crew as well. Sometimes they're looking for extra money and want to work on the weekend, but I let them decide that for themselves. I want them to have a reasonable balance between their home life and their work life.

What's the best part of your job?

Did you ever see the movie *The Replacements* where Keanu Reeves says what he fears is quicksand? When things go awry and you're just sinking into the ground? When I walk into a client's house and I can see that they're sinking in quicksand, I know I can help them get through this period of their life. My clientele—half of them are senior citizens who are leaving a home they haven't left in more than thirty years. They've hit the point where the stress of thinking through and solving the logistical problems of moving has brought them to the point of near despair. I'm able to go in and pull them back from that edge. People think of moving as a physical job. But the front end of this job is purely emotional. Customers need to be confident that they'll be able to start their new life and look back on this experience as a positive one.

There are a couple of things we do to help. One is that we have a secondhand store—we have clients with a five-bedroom home who are downsizing and going into retirement. Despite that, they can't deal with the fact that they have excess furniture. If it solves a problem for them, they can send furniture to the consignment store. It's not really a revenue-generating entity—the store hasn't made money in five years. It's there to solve a major emotional problem for our clients. We help them out through that process.

Sometimes we'll walk in and see a client who, despite their best efforts, is in a situation where there's a four-day difference between the closing on the house they're selling and the closing on the house they're buying. We maintain the largest fleet of trucks in New Hampshire, so we can load their belongings in a truck and just keep it in the truck until they can move into the new house. We want to give them tools of empowerment, so they can solve these problems.

What's the most challenging part of your job?
Last-minute changes by clients. Going back to trying to match our crew to the size of the job, on a number of occasions, we'll have clients who think that they'll dispose of 30 to 40 percent of what they have in their current house prior to moving day. Then they don't. When my crew shows up, I now have a job that is much larger than the crew I've allocated. Sometimes we can't find part-timers or pull people from another job. Then I have a crew that's pushed harder than I'd like them to be, and my empathy for them puts me in distress.

What's the most surprising thing about your job?
The State of New Hampshire social services and safety net is inadequate in a lot of ways. Our country is experiencing a crisis of many clients who have memory- or cognitive-related problems. So we'll be called in to try to help someone move who is experiencing that, and they have virtually no support. They no longer have the ability to make rational decisions. For example, I had a client who was a senior woman, a widow, who wanted me to move her to my warehouse. She knew she needed to leave her current environment, and she asked me to move her to my warehouse. I explained to her as gently as I could that she couldn't do that. She understood in the moment, but six hours later she called and asked when she'd be moving to the warehouse. I called every agency I could think of and could find no help for this woman. I have a hard time sleeping at night when I think about that. She had been a teacher in the state of New Hampshire for thirty-eight years.

How did (or didn't) your education prepare you for this job?
I went to the College of Insurance in Manhattan [New York City]. My discipline was finance and insurance underwriting. Once I entered the business arena, I needed to learn a set of skills that typically are not taught in college. What I drew from my education was that I needed to be a lifelong learner. I needed to self-assign topics to learn along the way. In my prior career, I created a national brand for insurance. I had no prior knowledge or education of how to do that. I went out and drew on every resource I could to teach myself how to do that. From my formal education

I learned the process of learning and that I had to be solely responsible for my learning thereafter. I believe that all learning is pulled, not pushed. When the student is interested in the topic, you have genuine education. When it's assigned, they have to determine how much they have to do get through it. That does less to help them in the long term. So I knew the process from a macro level of what I needed to learn and how I needed to learn it. I did financial modeling for many years, so when I took on this business, I built models to understand the dynamics of the business. There's a spreadsheet called the Monte Carlo Simulation that ranks variables from the most desirable outcome to the least. That helped me dial into the elements of this business that would make it successful versus unsuccessful.

Is owning/running a moving and storage company what you expected?

The answer would clearly be *no.* The situation I described with the retired teacher blindsided me. In the office type environment I was in, I never was exposed to that type of element at all. To show up and be in direct contact with the situation and realize the implications of what is actually happening—I wasn't ready for that.

What's next for the company? Where do you see yourself going from here?

On a macro scale, we're looking at the future development of storage within our business. Right now, we have a 32,000-square-foot warehouse. In spring, I'm going to add a couple hundred self-storage units. I may also purchase storage containers for on-site storage. That would be a lateral incubation of different parts of the business—expanding by going into complementary "peer-level" type businesses. That allows me to use the infrastructure I currently have more efficiently.

What is your advice for someone considering this career?

Start with empathy. The clientele that we come in contact with are in such a vulnerable state and have heard stories of movers who have taken advantage of other people, so if you approach it from a standpoint of empathy, where you're giving the proper assurances in the right way and matching that with consumer ratings online that give them assurances that what you're saying is actually true, you've entered a field where you can provide a service in a way that is extraordinarily meaningful for the client. The lesson of not creating "work widows" may have to be learned the hard way—at least it was in my case!

For CDL drivers who drive a tractor-trailer, when they travel interstate, they're effectively camping out in their trucks. They're using public showers, public toilets. One of the advantages of working for an independent moving company is quality of life. When we send our crew on interstate trips, they're staying at business-level hotels, eating in restaurants that are not truck stops, which typically only offer unhealthy food choices, and they're not overscheduled. A traditional trucking company can only make money by overscheduling their employees. That doesn't happen here.

Long-haul truckers have extremely high divorce rates. They're on the road in grueling conditions for long periods of time. When they return home, they're mentally and physically shell-shocked. It makes their home life difficult because they're work life is difficult. We try to find that balance in between. When I was working sixty to seventy hours a week, when I was home, I wasn't there—I was a ghost. When you're traveling out of state with a truck, you may only be driving for eleven hours, but you're on duty twenty-four hours a day because you can't abandon your truck.

Notes

Introduction

1. Blume Global, "The Supply Chain, Explained," https://www.blumeglobal .com/learning/supply-chain-explained/.

2. Blume Global, "The Supply Chain, Explained."

3. Kristina Zucchi, "Job Description and Salary: Supply Chain Management," *Investopedia/Careers/Salaries and Compensation*, March 30, 2019, https://www.investo pedia.com/articles/personal-finance/021015/job-description-and-salary-supply -chain-management.asp.

4. Walt Whitman, "Song of the Open Road," in *Leaves of Grass* (Brooklyn, NY, 1856).

Chapter 1

1. U.S. Bureau of Labor Statistics, "What Bus Drivers Do," *Occupational Outlook Handbook*, last modified December 11, 2019, https://www.bls.gov/ooh/transporta tion-and-material-moving/bus-drivers.htm#tab-2.

2. Federal Motor Carrier Safety Administration (FMCSA), "Driver Medical Fitness for Duty," last updated December 17, 2019, https://www.fmcsa.dot.gov/medical /driver-medical-requirements/driver-medical-fitness-duty.

3. U.S. Bureau of Labor Statistics, "Delivery Truck Drivers and Driver/Sales Workers: Work Environment," *Occupational Outlook Handbook*, last modified September 1, 2020, https://www.bls.gov/ooh/transportation-and-material-moving /delivery-truck-drivers-and-driver-sales-workers.htm.

4. U.S. Bureau of Labor Statistics, "Delivery Truck Drivers and Driver/Sales Workers."

5. "What Is a Regional Truck Driver?" *Schneider.com*, 2021, https://schneider jobs.com/truck-driving-jobs/driving-opportunities/regional.

6. Bob Costello and Alan Karickhoff, "Truck Driver Shortage Analysis 2019," *American Trucking Association*, July 2019, https://www.trucking.org/sites/default/files/2020-01/ATAs%20Driver%20Shortage%20Report%202019%20with%20cover.pdf.

7. U.S. Bureau of Labor Statistics, "Heavy and Tractor-Trailer Truck Drivers: Work Environment," *Occupational Outlook Handbook*, last modified September 16, 2020, https://www.bls.gov/ooh/transportation-and-material-moving/heavy-and-tractor-trailer-truck-drivers.htm#tab-3.

8. Adam Hayes, "Distribution Management," *Investopedia*, November 13, 2020, https://www.investopedia.com/terms/d/distribution-management.asp.

9. U.S. Bureau of Labor Statistics, "Logisticians: Job Outlook," *Occupational Outlook Handbook*, last modified September 16, 2020, https://www.bls.gov/ooh/business-and-financial/logisticians.htm#tab-6.

10. Kristina Zucchi, "Job Description and Salary: Supply Chain Management," *Investopedia/Careers/Salaries and Compensation*, March 30, 2019, https://www.investopedia.com/articles/personal-finance/021015/job-description-and-salary-supply-chain-management.asp.

11. U.S. Bureau of Labor Statistics, "What Industrial Engineers Do," *Occupational Outlook Handbook*, last modified September 21, 2020, https://www.bls.gov/ooh/architecture-and-engineering/industrial-engineers.htm#tab-2.

12. U.S. Bureau of Labor Statistics, "Industrial Engineers: Job Outlook," *Occupational Outlook Handbook*, last modified September 21, 2020, https://www.bls.gov/ooh/architecture-and-engineering/industrial-engineers.htm#tab-6.

13. "Clerk Inventory Salary in the United States," *Salary.com*, December 28, 2020, https://www.salary.com/research/salary/listing/clerk-inventory-salary.

14. "Hourly Wage for Production Clerk Salary in the United States," *Salary.com*, December 28, 2020, https://www.salary.com/research/salary/listing/production-clerk-hourly-wages.

15. "Logistics Assistant II Salary in the United States," *Salary.com*, December 28, 2020, https://www.salary.com/research/salary/alternate/logistics-assistant-ii-salary.

16. "Operations and Supply Chain Manager Salaries," *Glassdoor*, January 25, 2021, https://www.glassdoor.com/Salaries/operations-and-supply-chain-manager-salary-SRCH_KO0,35.htm.

17. "Average Customer Service Representative (CSR) with Supply Chain Skills Salary," *PayScale*, May 5, 2018, https://www.payscale.com/research/US/Job=Customer_Service_Representative_(CSR)/Salary/4e41cb63/Supply-Chain.

18. "How Much Does a Purchasing Agent Earn in the United States?" *Zippia*, December 21, 2020, https://www.zippia.com/purchasing-agent-jobs/salary/.

19. "Transportation Specialist Salary in the United States," *Salary.com*, 2020, https://www.salary.com/research/salary/listing/transportation-specialist-salary.

20. "Logistics Specialist Salary in the United States," *Salary.com*, December 28, 2020, https://www.salary.com/research/salary/posting/logistics-specialist-salary.

Chapter 2

1. William H. McCraven, *Make Your Bed: Little Things That Can Change Your Life . . . and Maybe the World* (New York: Grand Central, 2017).

2. Courtney Connley, "Here's What Making Your Bed (or Not) Reveals about Your Personality," *Make It: Careers* (blog), September 13, 2018, https://www.cnbc.com/2018/09/12/heres-what-making-your-bed-or-not-reveals-about-your-personality.html.

3. Brian Tracy, "Good Habits Worth Developing: 3 Things Hard-Working and Successful People Do Differently," *Brian Tracy International*, https://www.briantracy.com/blog/personal-success/good-habits-worth-developing-3-things-hard-working-and-successful-people-do-differently/.

4. U.S. Bureau of Labor Statistics, "Taxi Drivers, Ride-Hailing Drivers, and Chauffeurs: Pay," *Occupational Outlook Handbook*, last modified September 4, 2019, https://www.bls.gov/ooh/transportation-and-material-moving/taxi-drivers-and-chauffeurs.htm#tab-5.

5. U.S. Bureau of Labor Statistics, "Taxi Drivers, Ride-Hailing Drivers, and Chauffeurs: Pay."

6. Maria LaMagna, "This Is How Much Uber Drivers Really Make," *MarketWatch*, May 15, 2018, https://www.marketwatch.com/story/this-is-how-much-uber-drivers-really-make-2018-05-15.

7. U.S. Bureau of Labor Statistics, "Bus Drivers: Pay," *Occupational Outlook Handbook*, last modified December 11, 2019, https://www.bls.gov/ooh/transportation-and-material-moving/bus-drivers.htm#tab-5.

8. "Regional Truck Driver Salary," *ZipRecruiter*, January 19, 2021, https://www.ziprecruiter.com/Salaries/Regional-Truck-Driver-Salary.

9. Sean Kilcarr, "Truck Driver Satisfaction Isn't All about Pay," *FleetOwner.com*, October 16, 2017, https://www.fleetowner.com/industry-perspectives/trucks-at-work/article/21701192/truck-driver-satisfaction-isnt-all-about-pay.

10. U.S. Bureau of Labor Statistics, "Heavy and Tractor-Trailer Truck Drivers: Pay," *Occupational Outlook Handbook*, last modified September 16, 2020, https://www

.bls.gov/ooh/transportation-and-material-moving/heavy-and-tractor-trailer-truck
-drivers.htm#tab-5.

11. U.S. Bureau of Labor Statistics, "Logisticians: Pay," *Occupational Outlook Handbook*, last modified February 17, 2021, https://www.bls.gov/ooh/business-and -financial/logisticians.htm#tab-5.

12. "Supply Chain Manager Salaries in United States," *Glassdoor*, January 5, 2021, https://www.glassdoor.ca/Salaries/us-supply-chain-manager-salary-SRCH_IL.0,2 _IN1_KO3,23.htm.

13. U.S. Bureau of Labor Statistics, "How to Become an Industrial Engineer," *Occupational Outlook Handbook*, last modified September 21, 2020, https://www.bls .gov/ooh/architecture-and-engineering/industrial-engineers.htm#tab-4.

14. U.S. Bureau of Labor Statistics, "Industrial Engineers: Pay," *Occupational Outlook Handbook*, last modified September 21, 2020, https://www.bls.gov/ooh/archi tecture-and-engineering/industrial-engineers.htm#tab-5.

Chapter 3

1. City of Manchester, New Hampshire, "Taxi License," 2021, https://www.man chesternh.gov/Departments/City-Clerk/Licenses-and-Permits/Taxi-License.

2. New York State Department of Motor Vehicles, "Get a CDL," 2021, https:// dmv.ny.gov/get-cdl.

3. MetroWest Regional Transit Authority, "Commercial Driver's License," 2021, https://www.mwrta.com/programs/commercial-drivers-license.

4. Monterey County Office of Education, "Driver Requirements," 2021, https:// www.montereycoe.org/programs-services/transportation/driver-requirements/.

5. Monterey County Office of Education, "Driver Requirements."

6. Vermont Agency of Transportation, Department of Motor Vehicles, "Commercial Driver's License (CDL) & Permit (CLP)," 2021, https://dmv.vermont .gov/licenses/types-of-licenses-ids/commercial-drivers-license-cdl.

7. Charlotte Kirkwood, "Requirements for Getting a Chauffeur's Driver's License in Texas," *Career Trend*, December 28, 2018, https://careertrend.com/info-8628519 -kind-need-drive-limo-pennsylvania.html.

8. "Transportation Majors and Undergraduate Degrees," *Study.com*, April 24, 2020, https://study.com/transportation_major.html.

9. Association for Supply Chain Management, *2020 Supply Chain Salary and Career Survey Report*, 2020, https://www.ascm.org/globalassets/documents--files/salary -survey/2020-salary-report.pdf.

10. Association for Supply Chain Management, *2020 Supply Chain Salary and Career Survey Report*.

11. Jennifer Ma, Matea Pender, and C. J. Libassi, *Trends in College Pricing and Student Aid 2020* (New York: College Board, 2020), 10. https://research.collegeboard.org/pdf/trends-college-pricing-student-aid-2020.pdf.

Chapter 4

1. Ronald Kimmons, "What Is Required for a Company That Employs CDL Drivers?" *Chron*, https://smallbusiness.chron.com/licensed-child-care-3011.html.

Glossary

associate degree: academic degree granted after a two-year course of study, usually from a community/junior college, technical college, or trade school.

bachelor's degree: academic degree awarded to a person by a college or university after completion of an undergraduate degree program (usually four years); also called a baccalaureate degree.

benefits: various types of non-wage compensation received by employees in addition to their normal wages or salaries, such as retirement, health insurance, dental plan, life insurance, paid vacation and sick leave, family leave, and other benefits; also called "employee benefits."

blockchain technology: growing list of records (blocks) linked using cryptography.

bus: a large motor vehicle for carrying multiple passengers by road, serving the public on a fixed route for a fixed fare.

cam: part of an engine that works with the rotating camshaft to push valves open.

charter bus: a bus hired to transport specific large groups to specific locations for an agreed-upon fee; also called a motor coach.

chauffeur: professional driver hired to drive limousines, vans, or private cars.

Class A CDL: highest level of commercial driver's license; allows the holder to drive vehicles such as tractor-trailers (aka semi, big rig, eighteen-wheeler), truck and trailer combinations, tanker vehicles, livestock carriers, or flatbeds.

Class B CDL: middle level of commercial driver's license; allows the holder to drive vehicles such as straight trucks, large buses (city buses, tourist buses, and school buses) or segmented buses, box trucks (e.g., delivery trucks and furniture trucks), or dump trucks with small trailers.

Class C CDL: lowest level of commercial driver's license; allows the holder to drive single vehicles with a gross combined weight rating (GCWR) of less than 26,000 pounds or towing another vehicle that's less than 10,000 pounds, including passenger vans, small HazMat vehicles, or combination vehicles that don't require a Class A or B license.

commercial driver's license (CDL): document issued by the state that allows the holder to operate commercial vehicles; *see* Class A, B, C.

commercial learner's permit (CLP): document issued by the state that allows the holder to learn to operate commercial vehicles.

cover letter: business letter to introduce the material in an attached document, such as a résumé.

Department of Transportation (DOT): the federal government's lead agency for planning and support of the nation's land, air, and sea-based travel systems; each state also maintains its own Department of Transportation.

distribution management: an overarching term encompassing different aspects of overseeing the movement of goods from supplier or manufacturer to point of sale, including numerous activities such as packaging, inventory, warehousing, supply chain, and logistics.

electronic logging device (ELD): an electronic devise that synchronizes with a vehicle engine to automatically record driving time, for easier, more accurate hours of service (HOS) recording; mandated by congress to help create a safer work environment for drivers and make it easier and faster to accurately track, manage, and share records of duty status (RODS) data.

endorsement: qualification issued by the state allowing a CDL holder to transport certain kinds of goods, materials, or passengers.

extrovert: personality type characterized by outgoingness, high energy, and/ or talkativeness; a state of being where someone draws energy ("recharges") by being around other people.

FAFSA: abbreviation for the Free Application for Federal Student Aid.

Federal Motor Carrier Safety Administration (FMCSA): lead federal government agency responsible for regulating and providing safety oversight of commercial motor vehicles (CMVs); part of the U.S. Department of Transportation.

financial aid: money to help pay for college or training, includes grants, work-study, loans, and scholarships; may or may not need to be paid back.

gross combined weight rating (GCWR): total mass of a vehicle including all trailers.

gross vehicle weight rating (GVWR): maximum operating weight or mass of a vehicle according to the manufacturer specifications, including chassis, body, engine, engine fluids, fuel, accessories, driver, passengers and cargo but not trailers; also called gross vehicle mass (GVM).

ground transportation: system of transportation of people or goods via vehicles traveling on roads or highways.

intercity bus: a large motor vehicle for carrying multiple passengers between towns and cities on a regular route and schedule for a fixed fare (e.g., Greyhound, BoltBus).

Internet of Things (IoT): network of physical objects embedded with sensors, software, and other technologies in order to connect and exchange data with other devices and systems over the internet.

introverted: personality type characterized by a preference for individual or very small group pursuits; a state of being where someone draws energy ("recharges") by being alone.

local transit bus: a large motor vehicle for carrying multiple passengers by road and serving the public on a regular route and schedule for a fixed fare; usually owned and operated by a municipal transit company.

logistics: the detailed coordination of a complex operation that may involve multiple people, facilities, or supplies.

long haul: commercial transportation of goods over long distances, including across state lines and international borders.

paratransit van: vehicle that has been modified to serve people with disabilities; usually have special equipment such as wheelchair lifts.

PSI: abbreviation for pounds per square inch, a measurement of air under pressure; one PSI equals the force of one pound-force applied to an area of one square inch.

real-time inventory management: use of tools such as barcode scanners, inventory software, and such to digitally record inventory events instantly.

résumé: list showing an individual's education, training, and employment history, usually in reverse chronological order.

ride-hailing: service where independently contracted drivers use their own vehicles to transport passengers to locations of the passenger's choice; usually arranged with a ride-hailing company (e.g., Uber, Lyft) via an online app.

ride-sharing: situation in which people decide to ride together in a vehicle owned by one of them, usually the driver; also called carpooling.

school bus: vehicle for transporting groups of students from home to school, school to home, or to school-sponsored events; designed to be highly visible and include specific safety features.

short haul: commercial transportation of goods within a local or regional area.

supply chain: system of interconnected organizations, information, resources, and activities that work together to get products to consumers.

supply chain engineering: an engineering discipline concerning planning, design, and operation of supply chains using various areas in mathematical modeling; main areas include logistics, production, and pricing.

supply chain management: process of managing the flow modeling and services (i.e., movement and storage of raw materials, work-in-process inventory, and finished goods) from the point of origin to the point of consumption.

taxi: vehicle-for-hire that carries a single passenger or small group of passengers between locations of the passenger's choice; also called taxicab or cab.

USDOT number: unique number to identify transportation companies used by the FMCSA when reviewing compliance or when conducting inspections or investigations.

Further Resources

This section includes useful resources relating to ground transportation careers. While this is not a complete list of all the information out there, these resources will help you get started finding out more about the craft arts you're interested in. Note that some private companies are listed here because they provide useful information; however, a listing in this book does not constitute an endorsement of these companies by the author or the publisher.

General Resources

Bureau of Labor Statistics *Occupational Outlook Handbook*
An online, searchable database with extensive information on hundreds of
    jobs and careers, including different kinds of jobs in given fields, salary
    information, education and training requirements, projected demand, and
    much more.
https://www.bls.gov/ooh/

Schneider.com
Schneider is a company that provides transportation and logistics services.
    Their website has a lot of useful information for people who want to get
    into the field, such as *How to Become a Truck Driver: 3 Simple Steps to a
    Rewarding Career.* 2021.
https://schneiderjobs.com/truck-driving-jobs/inexperienced
    /become-truck-driver

Certification/Credentials

SUPPLY CHAIN MANAGEMENT

Certified in Production and Inventory Management (CPIM)
Demonstrates deep understanding of forecasting, master scheduling, materials
   management, production planning, and the extended supply chain.
https://www.ascm.org/learning-development/certifications-credentials/cpim

Certified Professional in Supply Management® (CPSM)
A globally recognized credential from the Institute for Supply Management
   (ISM) that demonstrates competence in sixteen important areas.
https://www.ismworld.org/certification-and-training/certification/cpsm/

Certified Supply Chain Professional (CSCP)
Shows that you understand the essential concepts, strategies, and technology
   affecting the extended supply chain.
https://www.ascm.org/learning-development/certifications-credentials/cscp/

COMMERCIAL DRIVER'S LICENSE (CDL)

Types of CDL Licenses: A, B, and C Licenses Covered
Andrei Zakhareuski explains the different types of commercial driver's licenses and the commercial learner's permit. From *Beginner Driver's Guide*,
   Driving-Tests.org.
https://driving-tests.org/cdl-classification-licenses/

CDL Permit Test Study Guide and Cheat Sheet
From TruckingTruth.com: Ninety-three tips to help you study for your CDL
   permit test.
https://www.truckingtruth.com/wiki/topic-66/cdl-permit-test-study
   -guide-and-cheat-sheet

How to Get Your CDL—the Complete Guide
From TruckingTruth.com: Useful information that new truck drivers need to
   know about the requirements for a CDL.
https://www.truckingtruth.com/wiki/topic-39/cdl

7 Steps on How to Get Your CDL

This blog post from the Schneider Guy provides a quick overview of what you
need to do to get a commercial driver's license.
https://schneiderjobs.com/blog/how-to-get-cdl

DOT Physical Exam

6 Tips on How to Pass a DOT Physical

This blog post from the Schneider Guy provides a quick overview of the DOT
physical and what you need to do to pass.
https://schneiderjobs.com/blog/how-to-pass-dot-physical

Federal Motor Carrier Safety Administration (FMCSA) website.

https://www.fmcsa.dot.gov/medical/driver-medical-requirements/driver
-medical-fitness-duty

Healthline.com

Whelan, Corey. "What Is a DOT Physical?" *Healthline*. April 29, 2020. https://
www.healthline.com/health/what-is-a-dot-physical.

Education and Financial Aid

Learn more about going to college and scholarship options at these websites:

American Indian College Fund

Provides scholarships and college information for Native American students at
any of the nation's thirty-three accredited tribal colleges and universities.
https://collegefund.org/

American Indian Graduate Center & AIGCS

Scholarship for Native American students in the United States, at the high
school, undergraduate, and graduate level.
https://www.aigcs.org/

APIA Scholars

Nonprofit organization that provides college scholarships for Asian Americans and Pacific Islanders (AAPI).

https://apiascholars.org/

Cappex

A free website where you can find out about colleges and merit aid scholarships.

https://www.cappex.com/

CashCourse

"Your real-life money guide." Financial information, education, and tools to help you learn about your financial options.

https://www.cashcourse.org

Chegg

Website with searchable information about scholarships and colleges.

https://www.chegg.com/

Dell Scholars Program

Scholarship and college-completion program that helps students succeed.

https://www.dellscholars.org/

Fastweb

Search website for research on scholarships, internships, colleges, and such.

https://www.fastweb.com

Gates Millennium Scholars

Provides scholarships to reduce barriers to college for African American, American Indian / Alaska Native, Asian Pacific Islander American, and Hispanic American students regardless of major.

https://gmsp.org/

GoCollege.com

Your Guide to Free Money—College Scholarships.

www.gocollege.com/financial-aid/scholarships/types/

HS Finder (Hispanic Scholarship Fund)
Helps Hispanic/Latinx students find scholarship information.
https://finder.hsf.net/

KnowHow2GO
Information on how to get ready and go to college, for middle school and high
  school students and veterans.
http://knowhow2go.acenet.edu/

National Society of High School Scholars (NSHSS)
Connects students with scholarships, college fairs, internships, career and leadership opportunities, partner discounts, and more. All students are eligible
  to apply for high school and college scholarships in the areas of academic
  excellence, entrepreneurship, leadership, literature, medicine, music,
  STEM, sustainability, visual arts, and more.
https://www.nshss.org

Peerlift
Information about scholarships, internships, summer programs, and more
  gathered by students.
http://www.peerlift.org

Scholar Snapp
Free data standard allowing students to reuse their application information for
  multiple scholarship applications.
https://www.scholarsnapp.org

Scholarship America
Research and apply for scholarships from this website.
https://scholarshipamerica.org/

Scholarships.com
Free website to search for college scholarship and financial aid information.
https://www.scholarships.com/

Scholly
Mobile app to find scholarships for college.
https://myscholly.com

Thurgood Marshall College Fund
Provides scholarships for students at any of the forty-seven public Historically
    Black Colleges and Universities (HBCUs), as well as support for the insti-
    tutions. Occasionally, they offer scholarships to students at other schools.
https://www.tmcf.org/

UNCF
Awards scholarships and internships to students from low- and moderate-
    income families for college tuition, books, and room and board. Their
    website also has great tips on applying for other scholarships.
https://uncf.org/

Professional Organizations

Membership in a professional organization is a way to connect with other
people in your field, learn the latest information through conferences and pub-
lications, and demonstrate your commitment to the field.

American Production and Inventory Control Society (APICS)
International association for operations management. Provides information to
    and about supply chain businesses and guidance on production, goods
    management, inventory, logistics, and purchasing.
http://www.apics.org/

Association for Supply Chain Management
A nonprofit professional organization supporting supply chain organizational
    leadership and innovation.
https://www.ascm.org/

Council of Supply Chain Management Professionals (CSCMP)

An international membership organization for supply chain professionals. Provides education and career advancement tools to members who work in supply chain consulting, finance, planning, logistics, transportation, manufacturing, purchasing, sales and marketing, warehousing, and third-party supply chain logistics.

https://cscmp.org/

International Warehouse Logistics Association (IWLA)

Association for those who work in efficient warehousing and goods transportation across international borders.

https://www.iwla.com/

Material Handling Association of America (MHIA)

Association for those in the equipment, systems, software, system integrators, and system simulators in the supply sector of big material handling and transportation.

https://www.mhi.org/

National Limousine Association (NLA)

A nonprofit professional organization dedicated to representing and furthering the interests of the luxury chauffeured ground transportation industry.

https://www.limo.org/

Teamsters

One of America's strongest unions, with the mission to protect drivers' interests. Their website lists union benefits, information for different industry divisions/sectors, and local chapters.

https://teamster.org/

Bibliography

Ajilon. "A List of Supply Chain Management Jobs and Their Duties." https:// www.ajilon.com/job-resources/supply-chain-management-jobs-and-duties/.

Association for Supply Chain Management. *2020 Supply Chain Salary and Career Survey Report*. 2020. https://www.ascm.org/globalassets/documents --files/salary-survey/2020-salary-report.pdf.

Blume Global. "The Supply Chain, Explained." https://www.blumeglobal .com/learning/supply-chain-explained/.

Bradley, Kate. "How Much to Tip a Cab Driver?" *USA Today Travel Tips* (blog). https://traveltips.usatoday.com/much-tip-cab-driver-61137.html.

Burnson, Patrick. "High Demand for Supply Chain Professionals in the Manufacturing and Retail Industries." *Supply Chain News*. September 15, 2016. https://www.supplychain247.com/article/high_demand_for_supply _chain_professionals_in_manufacturing_and_retail.

CDL Paid Training. "Companies Offering CDL Sponsored/Paid Training." *CDL.com*. 2021. https://www.cdl.com/cdl-truck-driving-schools/truck -driving-school-resources/employers-offering-paid-training.

City of Manchester, New Hampshire. "Taxi License." 2021. https://www .manchesternh.gov/Departments/City-Clerk/Licenses-and-Permits /Taxi-License.

Connley, Courtney. "Here's What Making Your Bed (or Not) Reveals about Your Personality." *Make It: Careers* (blog). September 13, 2018. https:// www.cnbc.com/2018/09/12/heres-what-making-your-bed-or-not-reveals -about-your-personality.html.

Costello, Bob, and Alan Karickhoff. "Truck Driver Shortage Analysis 2019." *American Trucking Association*. July 2019. https://www.trucking.org/sites /default/files/2020-01/ATAs%20Driver%20Shortage%20Report%20 2019%20with%20cover.pdf.

Council of Supply Chain Management Professionals (CSCMP). "Definitions of Supply Chain Management." *CSCMP Supply Chain Management Definitions and Glossary.* https://cscmp.org/CSCMP/Educate/SCM_Definitions _and_Glossary_of_Terms/CSCMP/Educate/SCM_Definitions_and _Glossary_of_Terms.aspx?hkey=60879588-f65f-4ab5-8c4b-6878815ef 921.

Federal Motor Carrier Safety Administration (FMCSA). "Do I Need a DOT Number?" Last updated December 31, 2020. https://www.fmcsa.dot.gov /registration/do-i-need-usdot-number.

———. "Driver Medical Fitness for Duty." Last updated December 17, 2019. https://www.fmcsa.dot.gov/medical/driver-medical-requirements /driver-medical-fitness-duty.

Gaille, Louise. "19 Biggest Pros and Cons of Being a Truck Driver." *Vittana .org Personal Finance Blog.* October 23, 2019. https://vittana.org /19-biggest-pros-and-cons-of-being-a-truck-driver.

Glassdoor. "Operations and Supply Chain Manager Salaries." January 25, 2021. https://www.glassdoor.com/Salaries/operations-and-supply-chain-manag er-salary-SRCH_KO0,35.htm.

———. "Supply Chain Manager Salaries in United States." January 5, 2021. https://www.glassdoor.ca/Salaries/us-supply-chain-manager-salary -SRCH_IL.0,2_IN1_KO3,23.htm.

Hartman, Dennis. "Types of Delivery Vehicles." *It Still Runs.* https://itstillruns .com/types-delivery-vehicles-5488825.html.

Hayes, Adam. "Distribution Management." *Investopedia.* November 13, 2020. https://www.investopedia.com/terms/d/distribution-management.asp.

Herzog, Will. "Ride-Hailing vs. Ride-Sharing: The Key Difference and Why It Matters." *Ecolane.* https://www.ecolane.com/blog/ride-hailing -vs.-ride-sharing-the-key-difference-and-why-it-matters.

Kilcarr, Sean. "Truck Driver Satisfaction Isn't All about Pay." *FleetOwner.com.* October 16, 2017. https://www.fleetowner.com/industry-perspectives /trucks-at-work/article/21701192/truck-driver-satisfaction-isnt -all-about-pay.

Kimmons, Ronald. "What Is Required for a Company That Employs CDL Drivers?" *Chron.* https://smallbusiness.chron.com/licensed-child-care-3011 .html.

Kirkwood, Charlotte. "Requirements for Getting a Chauffeur's Driver's License in Texas." *Career Trend.* December 28, 2018. https://careertrend.com/info -8628519-kind-need-drive-limo-pennsylvania.html.

LaMagna, Maria. "This Is How Much Uber Drivers Really Make." *MarketWatch.* May 15, 2018. https://www.marketwatch.com/story/this -is-how-much-uber-drivers-really-make-2018-05-15.

Ma, Jennifer, Matea Pender, and C. J. Libassi. *Trends in College Pricing and Student Aid 2020.* New York: College Board, 2020. https://research.col legeboard.org/pdf/trends-college-pricing-student-aid-2020.pdf.

McCraven, William H. *Make Your Bed: Little Things That Can Change Your Life . . . and Maybe the World.* New York: Grand Central, 2017.

MetroWest Regional Transit Authority. "Commercial Driver's License." 2021. https://www.mwrta.com/programs/commercial-drivers-license.

Monterey County Office of Education. "Driver Requirements." 2021. https://www.montereycoe.org/programs-services/transportation/driver -requirements/.

National Highway Traffic Safety Administration (NHTSA). "School Bus Safety." U.S. Department of Transportation. 2021. https://www.nhtsa .gov/road-safety/school-buses.

New York State Department of Motor Vehicles. "Get a CDL." 2021. https:// dmv.ny.gov/get-cdl.

North Carolina School Bus Safety Web. "Frequently Asked Questions." http:// www.ncbussafety.org/faqs.html.

160 Driving Academy. "Truck Driving Classes." 2021. https://www.160driving academy.com/truck-driving-classes/.

PayScale. "Average Customer Service Representative (CSR) with Supply Chain Skills Salary." May 5, 2018. https://www.payscale.com/research /US/Job=Customer_Service_Representative_(CSR)/Salary/4e41cb63 /Supply-Chain.

Salary.com. "Clerk Inventory Salary in the United States." December 28, 2020. https://www.salary.com/research/salary/listing/clerk-inventory-salary.

———. "Hourly Wage for Production Clerk Salary in the United States." December 28, 2020. https://www.salary.com/research/salary/listing /production-clerk-hourly-wages.

———. "Logistics Assistant II Salary in the United States." December 28, 2020. https://www.salary.com/research/salary/alternate/logistics-assistant-ii -salary.

———. "Logistics Specialist Salary in the United States." December 28, 2020. https://www.salary.com/research/salary/posting/logistics-specialist-salary.

———. "Transportation Specialist Salary in the United States." 2020. https:// www.salary.com/research/salary/listing/transportation-specialist-salary.

Samsara.com. "Everything You Need to Know about Short-Haul Trucking." August 4, 2020. https://www.samsara.com/guides/short-haul-trucking.

Schneider.com. "How to Become a Truck Driver: 3 Simple Steps to a Rewarding Career." https://schneiderjobs.com/truck-driving-jobs/inexperienced/be come-truck-driver.

———. "What Is a Regional Truck Driver?" 2021. https://schneiderjobs.com /truck-driving-jobs/driving-opportunities/regional.

Smarketing, Tara. "Difference between National, Regional, and Local Trucking." February 19, 2019. *Roane Transportation*. https://roanetrans.com/differ ence-between-national-regional-local-trucking/.

StateUniversity.com. "Distribution Manager Job Description, Career as a Distribution Manager, Salary, Employment." *Careers*. https://careers.state university.com/pages/651/Distribution-Manager.html.

Study.com. "Transportation Majors and Undergraduate Degrees." April 24, 2020. https://study.com/transportation_major.html.

Tracy, Brian. "Good Habits Worth Developing: 3 Things Hard-Working and Successful People Do Differently." *Brian Tracy International*. https://www .briantracy.com/blog/personal-success/good-habits-worth-developing-3 -things-hard-working-and-successful-people-do-differently/.

TruckingTruth. "CDL Permit Test Study Guide and Cheat Sheet." March 21, 2017. https://www.truckingtruth.com/wiki/topic-66/cdl-permit-test -study-guide-and-cheat-sheet.

———. "How to Get Your CDL—the Complete Guide." December 27, 2019. https://www.truckingtruth.com/wiki/topic-39/cdl.

U.S. Bureau of Labor Statistics. "Bus Drivers: Pay." *Occupational Outlook Handbook*. Last modified December 11, 2019. https://www.bls.gov/ooh /transportation-and-material-moving/bus-drivers.htm#tab-5.

———. "Delivery Truck Drivers and Driver/Sales Workers: Job Outlook." *Occupational Outlook Handbook*. Last modified September 1, 2020.

https://www.bls.gov/ooh/transportation-and-material-moving/delivery
-truck-drivers-and-driver-sales-workers.htm#tab-6.

———. "Delivery Truck Drivers and Driver/Sales Workers: Work
Environment." *Occupational Outlook Handbook*. Last modified September
1, 2020. https://www.bls.gov/ooh/transportation-and-material-moving
/delivery-truck-drivers-and-driver-sales-workers.htm#tab-3.

———. "Heavy and Tractor-Trailer Truck Drivers: Pay." *Occupational Outlook
Handbook*. Last modified September 16, 2020. https://www.bls.gov/ooh
/transportation-and-material-moving/heavy-and-tractor-trailer-truck
-drivers.htm#tab-5.

———. "Heavy and Tractor-Trailer Truck Drivers: Work Environment."
Occupational Outlook Handbook. Last modified September 16, 2020.
https://www.bls.gov/ooh/transportation-and-material-moving/heavy-and
-tractor-trailer-truck-drivers.htm#tab-3.

———. "How to Become a Bus Driver." *Occupational Outlook Handbook*.
Last modified December 11, 2019. https://www.bls.gov/ooh/transporta
tion-and-material-moving/bus-drivers.htm#tab-5.

———. "How to Become an Industrial Engineer." *Occupational Outlook
Handbook*. Last modified September 21, 2020. https://www.bls.gov/ooh
/architecture-and-engineering/industrial-engineers.htm#tab-4.

———. "Industrial Engineers: Job Outlook." *Occupational Outlook Handbook*.
Last modified September 21, 2020. https://www.bls.gov/ooh/architecture
-and-engineering/industrial-engineers.htm#tab-6.

———. "Industrial Engineers: Pay." *Occupational Outlook Handbook*. Last
modified September 21, 2020. https://www.bls.gov/ooh/architecture
-and-engineering/industrial-engineers.htm#tab-5.

———. "Logisticians: Job Outlook." *Occupational Outlook Handbook*. https://
www.bls.gov/ooh/business-and-financial/logisticians.htm#tab-6.

———. "Logisticians: Pay." *Occupational Outlook Handbook*. Last modified
February 17, 2021. https://www.bls.gov/ooh/business-and-financial/logis
ticians.htm#tab-5.

———. "Taxi Drivers, Ride-Hailing Drivers, and Chauffeurs: Pay."
Occupational Outlook Handbook. Last modified September 4, 2019.
https://www.bls.gov/ooh/transportation-and-material-moving/taxi-drivers
-and-chauffeurs.htm#tab-5.

———. "What Bus Drivers Do." *Occupational Outlook Handbook*. Last modified December 11, 2019. https://www.bls.gov/ooh/transportation-and-material-moving/bus-drivers.htm#tab-2.

———. "What Industrial Engineers Do." *Occupational Outlook Handbook*. Last modified September 21, 2020. https://www.bls.gov/ooh/architecture-and-engineering/industrial-engineers.htm#tab-2.

Vermont Agency of Transportation, Department of Motor Vehicles. "Commercial Driver's License (CDL) & Permit (CLP)." https://dmv.vermont.gov/licenses/types-of-licenses-ids/commercial-drivers-license-cdl.

Whelan, Corey. "What Is a DOT Physical?" *Healthline*. April 29, 2020. https://www.healthline.com/health/what-is-a-dot-physical.

Whitman, Walt. "Song of the Open Road." In *Leaves of Grass*. Brooklyn, NY, 1856.

Wikipedia. "Vehicle Weight: Gross Vehicle Weight Rating." https://en.wikipedia.org/wiki/Vehicle_weight.

Zakhareuski, Andrei. "Types of CDL Licenses: A, B, and C Licenses Covered." *Driving Tests. Beginner Driver's Guide*. January 12, 2021. https://driving-tests.org/cdl-classification-licenses/.

Zippia. "How Much Does a Purchasing Agent Earn in the United States?" December 21, 2020. https://www.zippia.com/purchasing-agent-jobs/salary/.

ZipRecruiter. "Regional Truck Driver Salary." January 19, 2021. https://www.ziprecruiter.com/Salaries/Regional-Truck-Driver-Salary.

Zucchi, Kristina. "Job Description and Salary: Supply Chain Management." *Investopedia/Careers/Salaries and Compensation*. March 30, 2019. https://www.investopedia.com/articles/personal-finance/021015/job-description-and-salary-supply-chain-management.asp.

About the Author

Marcia Santore is an author and artist from New England. She enjoys writing about interesting people and the fascinating things they do. She has written on many topics, including profiles of artists, scholars, scientists, and business-people. She has also illustrated and published several children's books. See her writing website at www.amalgamatedstory.com and her artwork at www .marciasantore.com.